Promoting
Active
Learning

Chet Meyers
Thomas B. Jones

Promoting
Active
Learning

*Strategies for
the College Classroom*

Jossey-Bass Publishers · San Francisco

Substantial discounts on bulk quantities of Jossey-Bass books are available to corporations, professional associations, and other organizations. For details and discount information, contact the special sales department at Jossey-Bass Inc., Publishers. (415) 433-1740; Fax (415) 433-0499.

For sales outside the United States, contact Maxwell Macmillan International Publishing Group, 866 Third Avenue, New York, New York 10022.

Manufactured in the United States of America

 The paper used in this book is acid-free and meets the State of California requirements for recycled paper (50 percent recycled waste, including 10 percent postconsumer waste), which are the strictest guidelines for recycled paper currently in use in the United States.

10% POST CONSUMER WASTE

The ink in this book is either soy- or vegetable-based and during the printing process emits fewer than half the volatile organic compounds (VOCs) emitted by petroleum-based ink.

Library of Congress Cataloging-in-Publication Data

Meyers, Chet, date.
    Promoting active learning : strategies for the college classroom / Chet Meyers, Thomas B. Jones.
        p.   cm. — (The Jossey-Bass higher and adult education series)
    Includes bibliographical references (p.) and index.
    ISBN 1-55542-524-0
    1. Active learning. 2. College teaching. I. Jones, T. B.
(Thomas B.) II. Title. III. Series
LB1027.23.M49   1993
378.1'25—dc20   92-41685
                                            CIP

FIRST EDITION
HB Printing   10 9 8 7 6 5 4 3 2 1   *Code 9324*

The Jossey-Bass
Higher and Adult Education Series

Contents

x

Preface

In writing introductions, authors should always imagine that inside even the most enthusiastic and charitable reader lurks the skeptic asking: "What's in it for me?" And answers to that question had better be concise and convincing. Briefly, then, here is what you will find in the chapters that follow.

Active Learning

This book advocates the use of active learning in the classroom. What is active learning? Without agonizing about possible redundancies (try for a minute to envision "passive learning"!), let us simply say that active learning is usually understood to stand in contrast to traditional classroom styles where teachers do most of the work and students remain passive. Part of our task in writing *Promoting Active Learning* is to offer a more positive definition of this term. As we see it, active learning provides opportunities for students to *talk and listen, read, write,* and *reflect* as they approach course content through problem-solving exercises, informal small groups, simulations, case studies, role playing, and other activities—all of which require students to *apply* what they are learning.

Active learning derives from two basic assumptions: (1) that learning is by nature an active endeavor and (2) that different people learn in different ways. Two teaching corollaries seem to follow from these assumptions: first, that students learn best when applying subject matter—in other words, learning by doing—and second, that teachers who rely exclusively on any one teaching approach often fail to get through to significant numbers of students. As a result, both teachers and students end up dissatisfied. By including active-learning strategies in our teaching, we increase the odds that students will leave our classrooms with more than a notebook full of "facts." Research does demonstrate that when we use information (for example, rehearse it or solve problems with it), we are more likely to retain it (Bransford, 1979). And when we involve students in activities that lead them to discuss, question, clarify, and write about course content, we not only foster better retention of subject matter but help expand students' thinking abilities as well.

In classes that include active-learning strategies, teaching and learning are more collaborative. The teacher ceases to be the center of attention, and traditionally passive students can assume a larger role in learning and applying most subject matter. Granted, students may need a little prodding and encouragement to get started with active learning. But they often take to it enthusiastically after experiencing the immediate feedback that is characteristic of active learning and discovering how their contributions are valued.

Another benefit of active learning is that it addresses some of the legitimate concerns voiced by women, culturally diverse students, and nontraditional-aged students. It encourages various ways of learning a subject; in so doing, it draws naturally on varied experiences from students' everyday lives. Because active learning frequently involves students in cooperative efforts—discussing, developing, and analyzing the contributions of others—rather than in isolated and competitive situations, the classroom becomes a more hospitable place for a variety of student perspectives. This context also invites teachers to reexamine old assumptions about the teaching and learning process and to try out new teaching strategies.

The book should help those among us who in theory accept the value of using different teaching strategies but in practice tend to stick with the tried and true. Why is it so hard to change? Part of the answer, suggested by Paul Pintrich, is that little has been done to translate the research on learning and cognition "into directly applicable information relevant to . . . classroom practice" (Pintrich, 1988, p. 72). *Promoting Active Learning* aims to bridge that gap between research and practice.

In the chapters that follow, readers will find some encouragement and practical teaching techniques to expand their teaching repertoires and to involve students more actively. Our focus is on easily adaptable teaching tools that have been proven in a variety of classroom sizes and environments, from the seminar room to the lecture hall. We draw on the experiences of several exceptional teachers who are devoted to active learning and practice it in different academic disciplines. Their teaching tips and examples communicate an enthusiasm for active learning and lend important insights into its problematic aspects.

But, enough of what this book will do. Here is what it will not do!

Readers will not find a diatribe against lecturing. Neither our enthusiasm for active learning nor the current vogue of the approach has blinded us to the value of good lectures. Good lectures justify themselves by dramatizing the "creation of knowledge" and by interpreting "that knowledge for listeners" (Corder, 1991). We believe that good lecturing can engage students in the learning process, and we gladly admit that students learn from inspired lecturers. We did. But we also strongly believe that a steady diet of lecturing leads to intellectual anemia. Lectures can be more engaging when they are punctuated with brief active-learning exercises that enhance retention and application. Students need more opportunities to discuss the information they are receiving, use it actively in class, and apply it to their everyday experiences.

Finally, readers who are a little suspicious of the phrase *active learning* should rest assured that adopting this approach to teaching does not require professional expertise in group dynamics, nor does it necessitate a "touchy-feelie" approach to teaching. We teach best when we play to our individual strengths, and not when we force ourselves to use teaching methods that feel embarrassing or uncomfortable. Still, we can all profit by expanding our present teaching abilities. Those readers who are somewhat reluctant to change traditional teaching practices can rest assured that the active-learning strategies in this book are well reasoned and down-to-earth and do not require specialized training or a personality make-over.

Background and Audience

A good part of this book's richness comes from conversations with colleagues in our own Minnesota State University system and around the country and from the classroom strategies and experiences they have shared with us. Yet while their knowledge is liberally sprinkled throughout these pages, *Promoting Active Learning* still is flavored with the relevant research on teaching and learning theory. We have tried to strike a balance between our enthusiasm for active learning and our scholarly obligations to ground its content in the teaching and learning literature. We wanted the book to be pithy and practical, rather than a detached, academic treatise on this exciting topic. We emphasize some of the most important as well as the most accessible resources and research on active learning.

This book derives mostly from the authors' individual struggles as teachers. We are always experimenting and trying to expand our repertoire of teaching approaches—sometimes successfully, sometimes not. What is more, most of our teaching experience has been at a university designed for adult students who expect to participate in their own learning. We have learned a lot from our students, and as a result, we continue to modify our own teaching strategies.

We think that what we have written will appeal to a variety of readers, from those already committed to active learning who want to expand the range of their teaching activities, to those who still need some background and encouragement as a prelude to changing their teaching strategies. While the main audience for the book is college teachers, it also has value for high school teachers, graduate students working as teaching assistants, and students enrolled in schools of education.

Overview of the Contents

Part One surveys the general subject of active learning and why it makes sense as a teaching strategy. Chapter One presents the case for active learning in light of changing concepts of teaching and an increasingly diverse student body. Chapter Two looks more closely at the nature of active learning and how it works. Chapter Three examines some of the details—such as clarifying course objectives, dealing with classroom space and the learning environment, first-class activities, and student surveys—essential to creating the positive atmosphere necessary for successful active learning.

Part Two considers four major active-learning teaching strategies. In Chapter Four, we center on informal small groups. The benefits and pitfalls of small groups, guidelines for behavior, ways to "size" groups for an activity, and methods of managing informal small-group activities are discussed here. Chapter Five focuses specifically on how cooperative student projects differ from informal small groups, what can happen in them, and how to start them successfully to enhance individual projects and graded group efforts. Chapter Six examines the concept of simulation and such varied strategies as role play, simulation exercises and games, and computer models. The ways in which simulation strategies challenge students' thinking and develop important learning skills are also probed. Chapter Seven completes the discussion of major active-learning strategies by providing a survey of the case study method, including overviews of how to prepare case materials and handle classroom discussions effectively.

Part Three explores how reading assignments, outside resource persons, and electronic media can be successfully matched with active-learning strategies in the classroom. Chapter Eight advises on ways to connect outside reading assignments to active-learning strategies inside the classroom. It also demonstrates how to go about locating and using outside resource persons in active-learning strategies, paying heed to how both visitors and students should be prepared for the experience. Chapter Nine suggests to readers creative uses for basic elements of electronic-teaching technology such as overhead projectors, videocassette cameras, and computers, spotlighting ways to get started and to use these devices in the service of active learning. Chapter Ten is a summary chapter, in which we consider these key questions: How does active learning fit with the larger goals of a liberal education? What are some of the practical steps teachers can take that will help ease the transition from a traditional lecture format to active learning? How do we know if our active-learning efforts really work?

Throughout this book, we emphasize the intimate, critical connection between writing, discussion, and active learning, rather than artificially isolating those issues in separate chapters. Readers should take note that Chapters Four through Nine contain some "teaching tips" and end with concrete models for translating ideas for active learning into practice. Finally, we have provided brief, annotated Selected Resources for Additional Reading, consisting of key readings related to the specific topics and strategies the book addresses.

Acknowledgments

Special thanks are due to several people for their help on this book. The academic vice president of Metropolitan State University, Leah Harvey, allowed us extra time away from some of our university duties in the summer quarter of 1990. A Bush Foundation grant to the Minnesota State University system also enabled us to spend time on aspects of this project. Our colleagues at Metropolitan State University and throughout the State University system contributed teaching tips and classroom models, as well as offering assistance in reading drafts and sharing some of their research findings. Specifically, we would like to thank Daniel Abebe, Frank Beil, Earl Bolick, Beverly Ferguson, Maythee Kantar, Suzanne Walfoort, Catherine Warrick, Katherine Wellington, and Fancher Wolfe from Metropolitan State University and Linda Urrutia Scott from St. Cloud University for reading and critiquing our initial drafts. Marcia Anderson helped us with research on special topics, and Elizabeth Houle provided invaluable assistance when our computers crashed. Our thanks to John Chaffee of LaGuardia Community College for reading an early draft and the final draft. Prudy Hall of Hiram College also read and commented on the entire manuscript. We also owe a tremendous debt to Maryellen Weimer of Pennsylvania State University and Lorenz Boehm of Oakton Community College for their close reading of the final manuscript and for their excellent suggestions.

Faculty colleagues who contributed teaching tips, teaching models, and other information about active-learning strategies are as follows: Carol Avelsgaard, Sharon Bailey-Bok, Earl Bolick, Larry Crockett, Sheryl Dowlin, Rob Erickson, Deanna Evans, Mike Galegher, Muriel Gilman, Patricia Heller, Mel Henderson, Carla Johnson, Loretta Johnson, Barbara Keating, Steve Klepetar, Art

Lee, Janet Lee, Judith Litterst, Alice Magnuson, Gabriel Manrique, Miriam Meyers, Denise Mitten, Thomas O'Toole, Mary Overvold-Ronnigen, Linda Peterson, Laurinda Porter, Sara Rasch, Catherine Ray, Bob Raymond, Roseanna Ross, Linda Urrutia Scott, Suzanne Stangl-Erkens, Louise Thoreson, Catherine Warrick, Anne Webb, and Fancher Wolfe.

Our deepest gratitude to our many students at Metropolitan State University, who taught us how to teach and—sometimes gently, at times not so gently—reminded us that their learning needs were as important as our teaching needs.

Finally, we would like to thank Miriam Meyers and Susan Nathan, whose challenges to our thinking and whose personal support have always sustained us far beyond this particular project.

Minneapolis, Minnesota   Chet Meyers
February 1993   Thomas B. Jones

The Authors

Chet Meyers is professor of humanities at Metropolitan State University in Minneapolis. He received his B.A. degree (1964) from Allegheny College in sociology and his M.Div. degree (1968) from Yale Divinity School. Meyers is one of the coordinators of the Teaching Center at Metropolitan State and has coordinated ongoing teaching seminars for faculty development. In addition to his work at Metropolitan State, he has led faculty development workshops at colleges and universities throughout the United States.

While Meyers's formal academic training is in the humanities, his informal training and interests are wide-ranging. He has taught courses in adult education, human services, philosophy, and freshwater fishing—a subject on which he has also written several books and articles. He has received recognition for his teaching excellence at his home university and in 1981 was awarded a Bush Foundation Fellowship to study approaches to teaching critical thinking. He is the author of *Teaching Students to Think Critically* (1986).

Thomas B. Jones is professor of humanities at Metropolitan State University in Minneapolis. He received his B.A. degree (1964) from the University of Minnesota in history, and his M.A. (1966) and Ph.D. (1968) degrees from Cornell University in American history. At Metropolitan State University, Jones teaches courses in American history and coordinates the history teaching faculty. In 1983, he was awarded a Bush Foundation Fellowship for a year of research and writing on liberal education and business study. His published works include writings on American history, the humanities, nontraditional education, and liberal learning for business students.

Promoting
Active
Learning

PART 1

Understanding Active Learning

ONE

The Case for
Active Learning

A subtle but important change is taking place in American higher education. Teachers are beginning to talk with each other about teaching and, as a result, to change the ways they teach. Though hardly a revolution, this conversation about teaching breaks a long tradition reflecting an almost feudal mentality in which teachers surrounded their classrooms with psychological moats and fortifications. The lords and ladies of academe seldom discussed what went on within their castles. And, when the teaching nobility did meet, their conversations revolved around research and discipline-related issues—not teaching. Happily, signs indicate a changing perspective.

One clear indication of changing times is the number of national conferences on teaching that advocate a shift from lecture to active learning. At these academic conferences, where professors traditionally have only read their papers, presenters now are asked to engage audiences in discussion. Faculty development programs and teaching centers aimed at expanding teaching repertoires are springing up on many campuses. Journals, newsletters, and books on college teaching are also increasingly available. Thus, a nationwide dialogue about the hows and whys, the nuts and bolts, of teaching is developing and promises to expand.

Why are college teachers willing to discuss their teaching experiences with each other more freely these days? And why are approaches to active learning so much a part of these discussions? There are no simple answers to these questions. However, in our conversations with colleagues around the country and at our university, we

3

sense at least two important forces at work that we will explore in this chapter. First, there is a growing uneasiness among teachers who feel that their old teaching methods simply do not work as well as they used to. This uneasiness is confirmed by a growing body of research on learning theory that challenges the traditional ways we think about teaching. Second, a changing student body in higher educa-tion—with differing expectations about teaching and differing learn-ing needs—calls into question the conventional wisdom about the teaching-learning process. Increasing numbers of working adults, women, and culturally diverse students in our classrooms have chal-lenged many of us to reconsider old assumptions and to start thinking about new approaches.

How We Think About Teaching

In the Athenian marketplace, Socrates nurtured some of the prom-inent roots of Western education as he questioned, prodded, and cajoled those who came to learn from him. Consistent with Plato's view of reality, Socrates' dialogues tried to *bring forth* from his followers a truth he believed they already possessed. This philos-ophy of learning ultimately gave way to something quite different, particularly as the modern university developed in Europe and in the United States. In part, as the result of the industrial revolution and an expanding body of knowledge about the physical world, professors no longer saw their role as Socratic midwives, laboring to bring forth knowledge from their students. Instead, they adopted a different approach, endeavoring to *deliver* knowledge directly to the uninitiated.

Given this "empty vessel" or "additive" theory of education, the evolution and predominance of the fifty-minute lecture seems natural. Although the commonsense wisdom of educators like John Dewey, Maria Montessori, and Alfred North Whitehead challenged this teaching orthodoxy, not until recently has sufficient empirical research on learning and cognition demonstrated some errors of our earlier pedagogical assumptions (Erickson, 1984; Bransford, 1979; Kolb, 1984).

Researchers on teaching and learning remind us that far from coming to our classes as "empty vessels," students arrive with their own perceptual frameworks intact (Erickson, 1984, p. 55). Of course, as we know from working with "difficult" students, these perceptual frameworks are not only intact, but often firmly entrenched. Researchers also teach us that people learn in different ways (Kolb, 1984; Briggs-Myers, 1980). Add to this the explosions of information and new insights that have challenged the traditional ways we think about our disciplines, and it is difficult, if not impossible, to think of teaching as merely passing on a static body of facts and figures to the uninitiated. As K. Patricia Cross reminds us: "Learning is not so much an additive process, with new learning simply piling up on top of existing knowledge, as it is an active, dynamic process in which the connections are constantly changing and the structure reformatted" (Cross, 1991, p. 9).

Changes in the ways we think about teaching are, perhaps, best reflected in the changing metaphors we use to talk about teaching. Richard Tiberius contrasts our older pedagogical metaphor of "transmission" with a newly developing metaphor of "dialogue" or "communication" (Tiberius, 1986). The transmission metaphor emphasized "the efficient flow of information down the pipeline," presumably to the empty vessel. In contrast, the dialogue metaphor emphasizes "the interactive, cooperative, relational aspects of teaching and learning" (Tiberius, 1986, p. 148). Transmission presumes a passive audience of individuals; dialogue assumes an active interchange among a community of learners and an intrinsic human learning capability.

Tiberius's description of changing perspectives about teaching and learning reflects the views of other contemporary educators. Parker J. Palmer, whose personal and humane conversations about teaching have attracted a large following, discusses the developing view of teaching as a shift in focus from the *individual* as the "agent of knowing" to learning as a *communal* act (Palmer, 1987). Transmission as a way of teaching makes sense so long as learning assumes a transaction simply between the teacher, as a source of "truth," and the student, as one in "ignorance." But, if learning is a dynamic process—an interchange that involves teacher and students as co-inquirers—then a communal dialogue is essential.

Palmer and Tiberius are not alone in their assessment and advocacy of a new way of thinking about teaching. For years, respected educators like Arthur Chickering, Zelda Gamson, K. Patricia Cross, Kenneth Eble, and Wilbert McKeachie have said much the same thing. Common to all is the idea that students learn not by just absorbing content (taking copious notes and studying for exams), but by critically analyzing, discussing, and using content in meaningful ways. As Pat Hutchings explained recently, "What matters . . . is not just what students know but what they can do with what they know. What's at stake is the capacity to perform, to put what one knows into practice" (Hutchings, 1990).

So it is clear that educators in this country are changing the ways they think about teaching and learning. One fundamental change has to do with teachers serving not only as sources of discipline expertise but as facilitators of learning. For many of us, this means reconsidering how we work with students in a classroom. Mary Field Belenky and her coauthors of *Women's Ways of Knowing* (1986) offer a metaphor reminiscent of Socrates. They suggest that our task as educators is to be "midwife-teachers" who help students give "birth to their own ideas, in making their own tacit knowledge explicit and elaborating it." Teachers should "support their students' thinking, but . . . not do the students' thinking for them or expect the students to think as they do" (Belenky, Clinchy, Goldberger, and Tarule, 1986, pp. 217–218). In this context of teachers serving as midwives and facilitators, active learning makes sense.

In Chapter Two we will talk more about the primary elements of active learning. In simple terms, it involves providing opportunities for students to meaningfully *talk and listen, write, read,* and *reflect* on the content, ideas, issues, and concerns of an academic subject. We think that these basic elements of active learning clearly dovetail with the changing ideas about education reflected by Palmer, Tiberius, Belenky, and others, all of whom seem to be calling for more active participation by students in the teaching-learning process. What may not be so clear is exactly how active learning addresses the needs of an increasingly diverse student body and how it relates to new research about student learning styles.

A Changing Student Body

The changing demographics of college students and what nontraditional students expect of higher education are beginning to have an impact on teachers' attitudes and the ways they teach. Adult students have increased substantially within the undergraduate population since the 1970s (Anderson, 1990). In contrast to traditional-aged students, adults are more vocal about their learning needs. Women and culturally diverse students are also growing in numbers on many campuses, bringing with them differing ideas and needs for their education that challenge old ways of teaching (National Center for Education Statistics, 1992). In response, educational reformers are busy attempting to make the curriculum more sensitive to the learning needs and styles of adults, women, and culturally diverse students. Let's consider adult students first.

Adults have had a tremendous impact on how we think about teaching because they differ from younger students in significant ways. Adults draw from a wealth of personal life experience. Often they have struggled, suffered, been broken and mended, and lived through situations that typical eighteen-year-olds have not. Many adults also return to school with backgrounds in leading, managing, and teaching others. Most have had to learn on the job and have participated in job-related training sessions. They are what Malcolm Knowles refers to as "self-directed learners" (Knowles, 1980).

Adults want to validate their past experiences and test them against what they are learning in college classrooms. They rightly feel that much of what they already know is important and should be used as a measuring stick for new learning. Thus, they often feel frustrated and discounted when they are lectured to and are denied opportunities to share their experience. To make this point clear, teachers might imagine a situation in which their roles were reversed. For example, it's doubtful that a philosophy teacher would sit mutely during a management training session on business ethics. It is equally absurd to expect a student who is a business executive to remain silent in an economics course.

Adults are experienced, tough-minded educational consumers who lead busy lives. Most work full-time, have families, are active members of civic and religious communities, and rarely waste their precious time on endeavors they think are worthless. They do not suffer fools gladly, and they would rather be actively involved in learning than sitting passively on the sidelines. Of course, sometimes adults will tolerate the "listen, take notes, give it back" game we too often demand of them, if that is their only option. More often than not, however, they are willing to speak up and voice their concerns. We know of occasions at our university, which is composed overwhelmingly of adults, where students have left their desks, walked out of class, and written to the dean requesting a tuition refund, citing inadequate and boring teaching as their reason. True, these students sometimes bolt out of classes for the wrong reasons—as when their cherished personal beliefs are challenged—but most often, their exits are an honest commentary on their exclusion from the teaching-learning experience.

While younger students most often remain silent, adults in the classroom will voice their frustrations and concerns. One colleague at Metropolitan State University got this message in her first quarter of teaching. While she was reading passages from Plato's *Republic* to her class, an older student in the back of the room stood up and respectfully, but forthrightly, said: "Professor, I believe we can all read what Plato has written. Now, if you will just help us discuss what he meant, we'll be getting somewhere."

When the assertive posture of adults is combined with the expectations of women, African Americans, Latinos, American Indians, Asian Americans, and other student groups that their concerns and experiences be included in higher education, powerful incentives for change result. Most of these students see the world through different lenses than those customarily used to construct the college curriculum. Though it is trite to say that a white, male, hierarchical system has dominated higher education, teaching too often has reflected an authoritarian, detached, and competitive style that leaves little room for the views of women and other cultures. The traditional classroom, in which professors talk and students listen, tightens the restraints of this dominant cultural straitjacket. Such an environment robs teachers of the opportunity to learn what women and students of color have to offer and disregards the fact that their intellectual development can take different forms as a function of their gender and culture.

The pioneering work on moral and cognitive development in the 1970s by Lawrence Kohlberg (1969) and William Perry (1970) gave us helpful concepts such as dualistic thinking and stages of intellectual growth. Kohlberg and Perry argue that students pass through stages of intellectual and ethical development, moving from a simple perception of the world in terms of right and wrong, good and bad, to an appreciation that life is not that simple because it involves a multiplicity of values and commitments. But this progression is unlikely to occur as long as teachers fail to challenge their students' dualistic world views by presenting alternatives. Indeed, the work of Kohlberg and Perry helped inspire educators to consider the value of active learning. The major weakness with their research was its focus on white, male students.

The work of Carol Gilligan (1982) and more recently, Belenky and her colleagues (Belenky, Clinchy, Goldberger, and Tarule, 1986), while supporting the general theory of intellectual stages, challenged Perry and Kohlberg by arguing that women have developed along different intellectual lines from men because of different value orientations. To these voices, we need to add the insights of researchers who are studying differences in learning styles among culturally diverse students in our society.

The research regarding the relationship between ethnicity and learning styles is far from conclusive. However, the evidence does suggest some connections. The most commonsense summary of this issue we came across is from James A. Banks (1988). He believes that the research indicates an important difference between students from African American and Mexican American cultures and their Anglo-American counterparts; that is, the former are generally more field sensitive in their learning styles (p. 465). Citing the work of Ramírez and Castañeda (1974), Banks relates that the terms *field sensitive* and *field independent* refer to two different styles of learning. One characteristic of field independent learners is that they "prefer to work independently while field sensitive learners like to work with others to achieve a common goal" (p. 459). If the research holds true, it suggests that some students

might do better in classrooms that use cooperative-learning strategies, as opposed to traditional competitive approaches.

It makes sense that cultural background has an impact on
learning style because the environment that surrounds us influences
how we come to learn. But Banks is cautious in his conclusions
because he realizes that research on cultural learning styles exhibits
little consistency from study to study, especially in terms of the
ethnicity, class, and gender of the individuals studied; statistical
methods of analysis; and variables used in measurement instru-
ments. What he fears is another kind of stereotyping that might
develop if teachers came to an oversimplified equation of ethnic or
social-class background and learning style. Banks concludes,
"Teachers should recognize that students bring a variety of learning, cognitive, and motivational styles to the classroom, and that
while certain characteristics are associated with specific ethnic and
social class groups, these characteristics are distributed throughout
the total student population" (p. 466).

In addition to research on cultural learning styles, studies of
cultural communication patterns suggest that students from some
cultures may not learn best where the communication pattern between teacher and student is usually one-way. Some of these students come from cultures with more interactive communication
patterns and rely on visual as well as verbal cues. Studies of American Indians, while acknowledging individual differences, suggest
that approaches to teaching that deemphasize the distinction between lecturer and audience, provide opportunities for collaborative
learning, tolerate some degree of silence, and include visual presentations of information and ideas, might make the classroom a more
hospitable learning environment (Kleinfeld, 1972; Boseker and Gordon, 1983; Browne and Bordeau, 1991).

This growing body of evidence only reinforces what most
teachers have experienced in their own lives: people learn in different ways and individuals can learn how to learn in a variety of ways.
The good news is that we do not need to be experts in learning
theory to put our practical experience into action. As Pat Burke
Guild and Stephen Garger suggest in *Marching to Different
Drummers:* "In some cases it may not be as important to know
exactly the style of each person we interact with as it is to act upon

the assumption that in any group of people a diversity of [learning] styles will be present" (Guild and Garger, 1985, p. 89).

Given all the new information on student learning, it is no wonder teachers are questioning their traditional methods and are talking seriously with each other about the "hows" of teaching. As Malcolm Knowles has observed, the changing American student body challenges some of the most treasured assumptions about teaching, including: (1) teachers should lecture and students should listen, (2) learning is a dispassionate, impersonal activity, (3) knowledge should be stored for future use, and (4) students have little to contribute to the learning process (Knowles, 1980, p. 45). Rather than despairing of this challenge, we should see it as an opportunity to reconsider personal teaching philosophies and to more actively engage our students in the learning enterprise.

But What About Traditional Students?

It appears that active learning has much to offer nontraditional and culturally diverse students. Yet what about the majority of students we teach—eighteen- to twenty-two-year-old students who, for the most part, may be white and middle class? Will they benefit from active-learning strategies in the classroom? The answer, we think, is a resounding "Yes!"

The decade of the 1980s witnessed a heavy barrage of criticisms from national and privately funded commissions on education, all calling for college teachers to more actively involve traditional-aged students in the teaching-learning process (National Commission on Education, 1983). Most college teachers are familiar with these ongoing criticisms. However, this time around, these critical reports and calls to action may be touching a deeper level of concern about today's college students. Faculty worry that students are less prepared for college study and more passive than ever in the classroom. Our own teaching experience makes us think so, and a number of studies help confirm it (Erickson and Strommer, 1991; Sedlack, Wheeler, Pallin, and Gusick, 1986).

We agree that traditional students are less prepared, and we are sympathetic when we hear others argue that most younger students are content as passive consumers of knowledge. As television critic Neil Postman contends, anyone who has spent over sixteen thousand hours huddled in front of a television set before entering a college classroom will not likely emerge from the experience unscathed by passivity (Postman, 1985, p. 4). Yet we remain optimists at heart. We believe that these students can and will take responsibility for their education, if we give them encouragement and opportunity (Erickson and Strommer, 1991). We also believe that this passive majority in classrooms and their poor academic skills are not solely a function of too much television, but are also the result of schooling and teaching methods that ignore genuine opportunities for engagement. As Bouton and Garth remind us: "There is only one way to acquire [academic] skills and abilities, and that is to practice them" (Bouton and Garth, 1983, p. 79).

A recent study by James Eison and Charles Bonwell dramatizes how little some teachers expect from their students in terms of active learning. A study of 125 students enrolled in sections of an American history survey course at Southeast Missouri State University reports that (1) 48 percent had not participated in small-group discussions, (2) 41 percent had not done short, in-class writing projects, and (3) 39 percent had not seen visual aids in class (Eison and Bonwell, 1988). Research of this nature helps explain why those of us committed to active learning often have trouble generating students' participation. Much of their previous college experience has reinforced their passivity.

Challenging passive students to be active learners and to practice academic skills does change the rules of the classroom and the teaching expectations with which students are most familiar. Nevertheless, we are convinced that somewhere, beneath the outwardly passive personas of that silent majority, lurks a mother lode of active learners, ready and eager to join in. Indeed, most of the teachers contributing to this book, who work directly with eighteen- to twenty-two-year-old students, have demonstrated that with the opportunity and proper encouragement, younger students will engage in their own learning and enjoy doing so.

Stepping Out of the Spotlight

By this time, you may agree that active learning makes pretty good sense, but a couple of questions probably linger, such as "What exactly is active learning?" and "How do I get started?"

We will postpone a full discussion of the question "What exactly is active learning?" until Chapter Two. However, generally speaking, almost any activity that substantially involves students with the course content through talking and listening, writing, reading, and reflecting counts as active learning. While the focus of this book is active learning in the classroom and specific classroom strategies (such as small-group activities, simulations, and case studies), the approach to teaching and learning we describe has a much wider field of play. Indeed, some of the most exciting active-learning opportunities take place outside the classroom through strategies such as internships, foreign travel, student study groups, and assessment of prior learning. But that is a subject that really deserves a book of its own.

Regarding the question "How do I get started?" the answer seems quite simple. Step out of the teaching spotlight! Let your students take more responsibility for their own education. Put them into situations where they must contribute to teaching themselves and others. As Alfred North Whitehead advised many years ago, let students develop the art of *using* knowledge (Whitehead, 1967, p. 1).

Of course, taking that step is easier said than done. Who wants to do it? You first!

We recognize from our own experiences that a number of powerful forces keep teachers front and center. After all, there are good reasons to lecture. William E. Cashin (1985) reminds us that lectures can:

- *Provide information* that is new, based on original research, and generally not found in textbooks and other printed sources
- *Highlight similarities and differences* between key concepts
- *Help communicate* the enthusiasm of teachers for their subjects
- *Model* how a particular discipline deals with questions of evidence, critical analysis, problem solving, and the like
- *Dramatize* important concepts and *share* personal insights
- *Organize* subject matter in a way that is best suited to a particular class and course objectives

College teachers in many disciplines argue convincingly, too, that a lecture approach is absolutely key for learning. Their argument goes that students need some background information, concepts, and methods *before* they can learn much on their own and become effective participants in classroom discussions. For example, a botany teacher might contend that students would not be ready to jump into small-group discussions about the potential impact of global warming without a lecture on the basic elements and principles of photosynthesis. Other teachers worry that if they do not lecture, their students will walk out at semester's end without a notebook full of key concepts, up-to-date information, and cultural legacies. As an example, historians might find it hard to whittle down what they consider essential knowledge about Athenian democracy or the Russian Revolution to spend valuable class time on active-learning strategies.

These are all legitimate concerns, and we do not mean to suggest that there are easy answers. We will address the inherent tension between covering content and using active-learning strategies in Chapter Three. But at this point, we do not want to create a false dichotomy between "good" active learning and "bad" traditional methods of teaching. What we need to remember is that the choice between lecture and active learning is not simply a case of either-or. Usually the problem is not a little reliance on lecture, but too much of it. As Eleanor Duckworth, quoting Dawkins, relates in "The Having of Wonderful Ideas" (1972), most of us are so busy "covering the material" that we miss the chance to "uncover it" with our students. We simply need to give students more time to dig beneath the surface, to grapple with the subject matter, and to make their own sense out of things. If we do, chances are they will be more likely to retain and use what we do give them.

What Teachers Would Rather Not Know

- While teachers are lecturing, students are not attending to what is being said 40 percent of the time (Pollio, 1984, p. 11).
- In the first ten minutes of lecture, students retain 70 percent of the information; in the last ten minutes, 20 percent (McKeachie, 1986, p. 72).
- Students lose their initial interest, and attention

levels continue to drop, as a lecture proceeds (Verner and Dickinson, 1967, pp. 90–91).

- Four months after taking an introductory psychology course, students knew only 8 percent more than a control group who had never taken the course (Rickard, Rogers, Ellis, and Beidleman, 1988, pp. 151–152).

We are not suggesting that lecture should be tossed out the window. Rather, we should season it with a greater variety of teaching strategies, so that students will share in the work of teaching and learning. For example, consider breaking students into small groups at the beginning of a class and asking them to determine what they felt was the main point of the last lecture. Then have the groups briefly report back on their findings. This provides an opportunity to clarify points of misunderstanding and is usually an enlightening exercise for students and teacher alike. We admit that it is risky to explore other ways of teaching, but the rewards can often outweigh the risks.

One reason why it is initially so difficult to try out new teaching strategies is that the old role of Lecturer as Knower of All is deeply ingrained in each of us. We have talked with colleagues who are committed to active learning and have shared the mutual guilt we feel while waiting for students who are completing small-group work or struggling to answer discussion questions. We know that these active-learning strategies work and that they can be more productive than traditional lecturing. But old teaching roles die hard, and we still feel guilty, as though we are not doing our job. Adopting active-learning strategies will cause some initial discomfort as we get used to new roles and teaching styles. Fortunately, new strategies can be explored without a complete pedagogical make-over.

Nothing is more phony—and more quickly rejected by students—than teachers trying on new teaching styles that fit uncomfortably with their personalities and abilities. Each of us teaches best when we play to our natural strengths. Active learning in the classroom makes possible a rich expression of personal strengths beyond a talent for lecture, such as leading discussions, provoking issues and questions, motivating and encouraging students, and creating activities and assignments that lead to discovery. Thus, while stepping out of the spotlight means less time for us at center stage, it in no way diminishes our importance in designing, choreographing, and managing the learning environment. Considering these teaching roles and appreciating their value in helping students learn assuages some of the guilt we may feel when we step down from the lectern.

One way to start thinking about adopting active-learning strategies is to assess our individual teaching resources. Perhaps we enjoy working with others and have some natural collaborative skills we could use to encourage cooperative student projects. Some of us may be good provocateurs and may enjoy involving students in classroom discussion and debate, thus making learning a process of mutual inquiry. Maybe some of us have always felt uncomfortable as experts behind a podium and feel better teaching in a less formal atmosphere. Here, we might adopt the strategy of less lecturing and more discussion and small-group exercises.

Whatever our personal resources, they can become a larger part of everyday teaching. In adopting new teaching strategies, we also can remain true to our individual strengths and our aims for education. Indeed, our case for active learning assumes that teachers can discover which teaching strategies will work best in their classrooms. And there is a growing body of literature that helps teachers explore new teaching strategies and assess their effectiveness. Thomas Angelo and K. Patricia Cross's work, *Classroom Assessment Techniques* (2nd ed., 1993), is popular with faculty attempting to assess their teaching strengths and weaknesses. Angelo and Cross suggest a number of short, informal methods of getting direct feedback from students on what they think about certain teaching methods—a topic we will return to in Chapter Ten. Also, at the end of this book, the Selected Resources for Additional Reading is an annotated bibliography of key active-learning resources you can use to see which strategies match your personal strengths and teaching styles. Our point here is to assure you that while there are risks in shifting from a traditional teaching role to one that allows more time for student activities, resources are available to help make that transition.

Final Thoughts

We have argued so far that changes in how we think about teaching, the growing diversity of our student body, and what researchers are discovering about the varieties of learning styles make a powerful case for active learning. Of course, embedded in our case for active learning are also some basic, personal beliefs about educating students. We will not preach, but we want to be explicit and make known our beliefs, as they are the driving force for us as teachers at a nontraditional, urban university. To summarize, we believe in encouraging students to be self-directed and collaborative, critically reflective, politically savvy, empathic, and fair-minded, as well as competent in the skills that are essential to meaningful lives and careers. We are confident that despite their sometimes passive, if not apathetic, exteriors, most students are capable of acquiring those abilities, because deep inside remains a desire to explore and to learn. Such students who learn to take responsibility for their own learning will help make our society more democratic and a better place for everyone. Finally, active learning helps prepare our students to be self-directed, lifelong learners—an ability they will all need in a society where individuals change jobs numerous times in their working years and have extended leisure time after retirement. We claim no originality here, as the sages and experts we cite and depend on throughout these pages attest. But we want to be clear that our personal commitment to active learning goes deeper than its efficiency as a teaching tool and that it is essential to our vision of what an educated person should be.

Those who agree that teaching is more than transmitting information to the uninitiated—merely filling "empty vessels"—and find some of our ideas and goals for teaching reasonable will agree that making room in their classes for a variety of active-learning strategies is a natural next step. Those who accept the premise that different students learn in different ways and are frustrated with not reaching their students by traditional teaching will find that active-learning strategies not only enliven the classroom but significantly improve their students' thinking and learning capabilities.

In following chapters, we will consider what is necessary to create a positive atmosphere for active learning and will then discuss a variety of teaching strategies. But as a necessary theoretical bridge to all that, we need to examine more closely the nature of active learning and how it works.

TWO

What Active Learning Is and How It Works

Typically, active learning is defined in contrast to the worst of traditional teaching in which teachers actively present information and students passively receive it. This definition says more about what active learning is not than about what it is. And since we know of no generally agreed-upon definition of active learning, we want to propose a working definition. In doing so, we hope to clarify for readers some of our assumptions about active learning's main features and also set the stage for a discussion of active-learning strategies. As we see it, active learning consists of three interrelated factors: basic elements, learning strategies, and teaching resources. In this chapter, we will explore the four *elements* (talking and listening, writing, reading, and reflecting) that singly or in combination are the building blocks common to all active-learning strategies. Then, in Part Two, we will expand on the *learning strategies* (small groups, case studies, and so on) that provide opportunities for students to learn and apply academic content. Finally, in Part Three, we will consider a variety of *teaching resources* (outside speakers, homework assignments, and so on) that can be used to enrich these learning strategies. Figure 2.1 illustrates the interrelationship of these three aspects. The *elements* of active learning, which we will discuss in this chapter, make up the building-block activities of specific *learning strategies. Teaching resources* represent additional sources that teachers can draw on to

Figure 2.1. Structure of Active Learning.

Elements

talking and listening

writing

reading

reflecting

↓

Learning Strategies

small groups   cooperative work   case studies   simulations

discussion teaching   problem solving   journal writing

↑

Teaching Resources

readings   homework assignments   outside speakers

teaching technology   prepared educational materials   commercial and educational television

---

enrich those learning strategies. Both the elements and the teaching resources contribute to the learning strategies.

A Pedagogy for Active Learning

As we have alluded to earlier, our primary assumptions about learning are that (1) learning is by its very nature an active process and (2) different people learn in different ways. We further assume that the process of education is about self-development and that learning is truly meaningful only when learners have taken knowledge and made it their own. We believe that, in many ways, learners construct their own knowledge. In this context, we find Piaget's concept of mental structures particularly helpful in our thinking about education (Piaget, 1976, p. 119). Piaget maintains that "children do not receive knowledge passively but rather discover and construct knowledge through activities. As children interact with their psychological and physical environments, they begin to form . . . structures of thought. These structures help to organize the child's experience and direct future interactions" (Meyers, 1986, p. 13). While we are not committed to the specific forms of intellectual development Piaget defined, we do agree with him about a basic principle of education: students, no matter what their age, need opportunities to engage in activities—with teachers, fellow students, and materials—that help them create their own mental structures and test them, thus making better sense of the world around them.

In this regard, we identify four key elements associated with active learning that we all use to create new mental structures: *talking and listening, reading, writing,* and *reflecting.* These elements involve cognitive activities that allow students to clarify, question, consolidate, and appropriate new knowledge. Each teaching strategy discussed in this book incorporates one or more of the key elements, or activities, as building blocks for constructing new knowledge. Nevertheless, we would be the first to admit that nothing is gained by simply having students talk, listen, write, read, or reflect—unless those activities are well structured and guided by teachers. There are sound pedagogical reasons for adopting active-learning strategies, and we are more likely to encourage students in those activities if we better understand how they work and how we can use them effectively.

In ways that we do not fully understand, the brain engages in different thinking processes, or operations, when we talk, listen, read, write, and reflect—an observation supported by research on teaching and learning. Thus, we need to consider the four elements of active learning in the context of some educational research and informed, practical observation.

Talking and Listening

In a society where silence is hard to come by and mindless chatter pervades our daily lives, some might ask, "Why not have students sit in silence for an entire class, listening to some *mindful* talk from their instructor?" Surely that makes more sense than having them jabber in small groups where they can only share their ignorance. Of course, students can and should learn from our insights as teachers; talk by teachers can be a valuable prelude to active learning. The problem, however, is not that teachers talk; it's that they talk too much.

A time comes when everyone needs to speak in order to clarify what they have heard, read, observed, or experienced. Simply put, talking clarifies thinking. We often experience this when we "talk things out" with a friend or colleague. The fact is, *we often do not know what we think until we try to say it.* And that is why talking with others is such an integral part of learning. When we are "musing quietly about something," as James Stice wisely remarks, our "thoughts can be rather woolly, and random thoughts about other matters can intrude." But when those thoughts are spoken, we must "organize and structure . . . comments so they make sense to the listener" (Stice, 1987, p. 103). The reason we need to provide time and activities for students to talk and listen to each other is that talking and listening discipline them to be clearer about their thinking.

Jack Lochhead and Arthur Whimbey (1987) are nationally recognized teaching experts who advocate having students follow a process of problem solving called Thinking Aloud Pair Problem Solving (TAPPS). Students in pairs "talk aloud" as one student attempts to solve a problem, while the other listens and tries to clarify what is being said. Thinking aloud works because it makes students aware of their thought processes as they solve problems; it also helps them quickly see when they make errors or run into blind alleys. In the TAPPS process, problem solvers must read the problem aloud and then talk about how they are thinking about solving it—verbalizing, whenever possible, all that they are thinking. Active listening is also a critical feature in this process, as it is the job of the listeners to understand which steps the problem solvers are taking and to encourage verbalization by asking questions, without stepping in and solving the problem (Lochhead and Whimbey, 1987, p. 75). Also, if knowledgeable students are paired with those who are struggling, a mentoring relationship develops that makes for more connected forms of learning. Xavier University in New Orleans has used the TAPPS process, in combination with an active-learning project entitled Stress on Analytical Reasoning, for a number of years. One measure of success for this approach is that Xavier, for a relatively small school, sends a disproportionately large number of African American students on to graduate education in the medical profession (Whimbey and others, 1980).

Opportunities for meaningful talk need not be as formally structured as the TAPPS approach. In classes of any size, teachers can form small groups of three or four students, for example, to summarize major points in a reading assignment. By putting things into their own words and listening to what others say, students will more fully comprehend what they have read. As Bouton and Garth (1983, p. 77) observe: "If learning involves the active construction of knowledge, then the process requires an opportunity to speak and to hear the response of others."

In addition to student-to-student conversation, teachers need to be available for in-class talk with students. As a spur to creating student-teacher dialogue during class time, consider the results of a recent three-year study of large lecture hall classes. Students surveyed felt that "the lack of instructor-student interaction, with opportunities for questions and discussion" stood as one of the biggest impediments to their learning (Wulff, Nyquist, and Abbott, 1987, p. 29).

Once we decide to take the risk by providing opportunities for students to talk with each other and with us, we need to model good communication skills in our teaching. In other words, students should see us doing what we expect of them. Therefore, we must listen attentively to their comments and questions and, when their intent is not clear, help them clarify and rephrase their thoughts. Again, let us emphasize that merely asking students to talk and listen to each other is no guarantee that significant learning will take place. Too often students are not really listening to each other, but are already composing what they want to say next. One way to make sure students are listening is to ask that they paraphrase back what they have just heard—before they start talking. In this way, they must practice active-listening skills, which are the flip side of mindful talking. In Chapter Four we offer some specific guidelines and models for structuring mindful talking in small groups.

Writing

Like talking, writing clarifies thinking. We write to communicate to a reader, even if it is ourselves, as in journal writing. Writing is an act of creation and clarification, as anyone knows who has labored over an article, a book, or even a departmental memorandum. The problem with most college writing assignments is that too often they call for students to merely rewrite what they have learned from lectures, or they ask for research papers summarizing the thoughts of others. The purpose of writing as a form of active learning, however, is to help students *explore their own thinking* about concepts and issues, thereby expanding their mental structures.

Writing can be a powerful prod to the expansion, modification, and creation of mental structures. Toby Fulwiler, a nationally respected writing educator, advises that writing "is an essential activity to create order from chaos, sense from nonsense, meaning from confusion: as such it is the heart of creative learning in both the arts and sciences" (Fulwiler, 1987, p. 44). Just like mindful talk, writing that is mindful requires discipline in sorting out thoughts, organizing them, and communicating them to another person. Part of the power of writing is that it requires so many kinds of mental operations. In "Writing as a Mode of Learning," Janet Emig (1977, p. 125) concludes: "If the most efficacious learning occurs when learning is reinforced, then writing—through its inherent reinforcing cycle involving hand, eye, and brain—marks a uniquely powerful multirepresentational mode of learning." Thus, writing can be a powerful tool for the active-learning classroom.

Thomas A. Angelo suggests a number of short, yet effective writing exercises that give instructors feedback on how well they are teaching, reveal what students are learning, and help students learn how to assess their own learning. Examples of short "minute writes" include (1) asking students the most important idea they remember from a day's lecture, (2) posing one question still uppermost in their mind, or (3) paraphrasing a key paragraph in last week's reading (Angelo, 1991, p. 2). The beauty of short writing exercises is that they work well in any class size, from the small seminar to the large lecture, and in disciplines from philosophy to chemistry. For example, William Zinsser (1988) relates how a chemistry professor regularly uses brief writing exercises as part of her multiple-choice exams. For a few selected questions, students receive no credit unless they choose the right answer *and* explain why it is correct. This technique gives teachers insights into how student thinking proceeds and reminds students that guessing their way through multiple-choice exams is not the best strategy.

We could argue further about the value of writing as a form of active learning, especially as students move from short writing exercises to more extended essays and research papers. But our main intent in this section is to underscore the value of writing as a means for students to clarify thinking and appropriate knowledge. We want to emphasize, as well, that the instructions teachers give for writing assignments have a direct bearing on results. Many students have constructed an image of what academic writing looks like (probably the result of too many reading assignments authored by academics who write poorly). Thus, when teachers assign papers, students naturally assume they are writing for someone who values that turgid, abstract, dispassionate, and even convoluted prose. What often results is the worst kind of gobbledygook, often combined with a few charming malapropisms. Interestingly enough, when we direct students to write for each other, they usually write with more clarity and precision. By structuring our assignments in what writing teachers call a "rhetorical context"—in other words, for a specific audience, situation, and purpose—we can free students from some of their misconceptions about college writing and help them write better.

We have asked students in our classes to write a summary paper, clarifying difficult concepts, addressed specifically to a friend who knows little about the topic assigned. These instructions immediately allow students to write in a more effective, conversational tone. At the same time, the refocused assignment helps us see if our students really understand what they are writing about. Creating a rhetorical context that is student-to-student, instead of student-to-teacher, usually results in writing that is clearer and less pretentious (Fulwiler, 1987, p. 51). Of course, there are times when students will still write with us as their primary audience. At these times, they can take for granted a common ground of knowledge they need not repeat for us, thereby moving more quickly to deeper levels of analysis.

Finally, no matter who the students' audience is, teachers need to give clear, specific instructions about the purpose of any writing assignment. And here many of us falter. According to Meyers, "When students are asked to 'analyze' or 'critique' . . . without knowing exactly what is intended by those terms, the results are predictably disappointing. Analyze in light of what? Critique from what perspective? The word 'analyze' might mean summarize, compare, contrast, take apart, reassemble, or regurgitate—in short it will mean different things to different students" (Meyers, 1986, p. 70). The point is obvious: avoid using words in assignments that we have not clearly explained to our students. One of the more helpful typologies of words for written assignments comes from Toby Fulwiler's book, *Teaching with Writing.* Here are some examples we might share with students so they know what we mean by certain terms:

> Analyze: Take apart and look at something closely.
>
> Compare: Look for similarities and differences; stress similarities.
>
> Contrast: Look for differences and similarities; stress differences. . . .
>
> Define: Explain exactly what something means.
>
> Describe: Show what something looks like, including physical features. . . .
>
> Evaluate: Make a value judgment according to some criteria (which it would be wise to make clear). . . .
>
> Justify: Argue in support of something; to find positive reasons. . . .
>
> Prove: Demonstrate correctness by use of logic, fact, or example. . . .
>
> Summarize: Pull together the main points.
>
> Synthesize: Combine or pull together pieces or concepts. . . .
>
> *Source:* Fulwiler, 1987, pp. 117–118. Used by permission.

Because most of our students are products of the television age, they generally do not come to our classrooms with much experience in writing. That is a simple fact, though we may bemoan it. Part of our task as teachers is to help students learn to write, so that they will become better thinkers. Nothing replaces writing as a unique mode of learning. As Zinsser (1988, p. 49) summarizes, writing "compels us by the repeated effort of language to go after the thoughts and to organize them and present them clearly. It forces us to keep asking, 'Am I saying what I want to say?' Very often the answer is 'No.' It's a useful piece of information."

Reading

Reading requires students to think in a different manner, because the object is to understand what others think, as opposed to primarily clarifying students' own thoughts by talking and writing. Critical reading involves students with some different tasks, such as scanning, identifying, sorting, and prioritizing information. In addition, reading calls for higher-level thinking skills, such as connecting ideas and sources of information, spotting faulty logic in argumentation, recognizing bias or hidden agendas, identifying unsupported ideas, understanding metaphorical levels of meaning, and entertaining other perspectives and points of view on a subject. For most of us, reading assignments are a fundamental resource and strategy for teaching students about our academic subjects. After all, the written text is still the primary material used in college classrooms. Thus we need to be active guides to ensure that students attend to the most important aspects of assigned readings.

Most of the research on reading comprehension deals with children in primary and secondary grades (Anderson and Pearson, 1984; Weinstein, Goetz, and Alexander, 1988), and the general findings will come as no shock. Under the domain of what reading researchers call "selective attention theory," we have learned that when secondary students have specific study questions before they start reading, they are more likely to recall that information (Anderson and Pearson, 1984, chap. 9). Similarly, the more explicit the instructions that teachers give for assigned readings (such as asking students to summarize the main points in an essay), the better students seem to do in comprehending what they have read (Winograd and Hare, 1988, pp. 126, 135).

Some of the best practical advice about making reading a meaningful exercise comes from Mortimer Adler's 1940 classic article, "How to Mark a Book." In it, Adler encourages readers to mark up their books—underline, highlight, circle key words, scrib-

ble comments in the margins—and to see this activity not as dese-
cration, but as an act of love. In a statement that prefigures what
research would only discover later, Adler comments on why writing
in books is so important: "The physical act of writing, with your
hand, brings words and sentences more sharply before your mind
and preserves them better in your memory" (Adler, 1940, p. 12). We
can help students learn what to highlight or notate by distributing
a brief selection from a text, asking a few key questions, and then
having students mark the reading, indicating key words and
phrases. Then we can show students how we would highlight the
same material by using an overhead transparency or handout of the
same selection. Because critical reading is so central to college learning, teachers should not take for granted that their students know
some of these most basic study skills.

    Chapter Eight is devoted to the topic of reading assignments
and active learning, so we do not want to spend more time here on
the subject. In that chapter, we suggest ways to motivate and guide
students' reading, such as previewing reading selections, identifying
specific types of reading assignments, and preparing study questions. Our point is that reading is such a fundamental learning
activity that we need to guide students' reading efforts and provide
some structure to those reading assignments. Too often we expect
that by simply having students do a certain amount of reading, our
objectives will be successfully accomplished. That is usually not the
case.

Reflecting

As much as college teachers profess to love the life of the mind, few
of our classrooms evidence an atmosphere of silent reflection. At the
same time, we all realize how important periods of quiet reflection
are as sources of insight in our personal and academic lives.
Though cognitive scientists have unraveled some of the mysteries
about how the brain works (Hunt, 1982), we still know precious
little about the significant processes of re-formation and consolida-
tion that occur when we quietly ponder something. We know even
less about those insights that come "out of the blue" when we are
not even aware of consciously thinking about something. However,

it seems natural that our brains need some quiet time to mull over, sort out, try to understand, and incorporate new information. As Jack Mezirow suggests (Mezirow and Associates, 1990), activities can be designed that involve higher-level learning processes and allow students to foster "critical reflection," which we take to mean the ability to identify and critique the preconceptions or seldom-tested assumptions that each of us brings to new learning experiences. Accordingly, the active-learning classroom should include exercises that encourage a healthy dose of quietude and reflection.

Piaget's insights about learning also support the need for reflection. Piagetian scholars Anton Lawson and John Renner (1975) stress disequilibrium and equilibrium as important processes in forming new mental structures. So long as new knowledge fits into our present mental structures, we are pretty much in a state of equilibrium. But when experiences and new knowledge do not fit within these structures, we encounter disequilibrium—a challenging and sometimes painful situation. Then, through a process of integration and appropriation, we either incorporate the new knowledge in our existing mental structures or construct new ones, thus returning to equilibrium. In a sense, the process of education is an ongoing dialectic between equilibrium and disequilibrium. For it to work, that dialectic must include some quiet time for reflection so that students can integrate and appropriate new knowledge.

If this Piagetian scenario is valid (and it makes sense to us), then we need to make room for reflection in our classes, especially following the presentation of new, challenging information that creates disequilibrium. By structuring opportunities for pondering and reflection, we can help students sort things out as they restructure old ways of thinking and move on to new understandings. In any significant learning experience, we cannot help profiting from time specifically set aside for reflection. At least that is what our personal experience as students and teachers suggests. We offer here a few simple examples of ways to build periods of reflection into teaching: silence in the classroom and student journals. We encourage our readers to think of other techniques by which they might accomplish the same goal, and to read works by others who are concerned with fostering critical reflection (Mezirow and Associates, 1990; Brookfield, 1987, 1990; Schön, 1987).

Silence in the Classroom

In *The Skillful Teacher,* Stephen Brookfield notes that students often complain when their teachers do not allow them enough time to simply think about things: "The period of mulling over, that is reportedly needed for learners to make interpretive sense of what is happening to them, is neglected" (Brookfield, 1990, p. 50). Perhaps we leave students no time to think things over because the amount of content we want to cover for the day supersedes anything else. Covering content too often rules out time necessary for reflection. How often do we ever say, "Well, class, I would like to spend more time covering the content of this chapter, but I am afraid we must stop here and spend a few minutes reflecting on what has been presented so far"?

As John Dewey so aptly observed: "All reflection involves, at some point, stopping external observations and reactions so that an idea may mature" (Dewey, [1910] 1982, p. 210). Periods of silence are necessary for ideas to mature. But as valuable a strategy as reflection might be, students (and teachers) often interpret silence in the classroom as something negative or even threatening. Teachers need to model and teach a more positive meaning for silence.

We can model silent reflection by pausing to consider students' questions, with attention to all they imply. We can also allow students more time to respond to our questions, rather than quickly and nervously seeking for answers to break the silence. Of course, giving students more time assumes that teachers are themselves comfortable with silence, which apparently many of us are not. One study of "wait time" indicated that the typical teacher pauses only 0.9 second (about the time of a butterfly's wing beat) between asking a question and supplying an answer when no hands shoot up ("Slow Down, You Move Too Fast," 1987). As an instructive experiment, get a stopwatch and take it to class next time. When you ask a question, punch the stopwatch on to see how long you can deal with silence as your students think about answers. Even five seconds may seem interminable. Waiting much longer for answers will be worth it, despite your growing itch to break in with an answer. When students have enough time to ponder, they can organize their thoughts for better answers, and some of those reticent students, who are normally not so quick on their feet, may surprise us with an answer if given the time.

Students can learn the "how-to's" of silence if we pause in the midst of a presentation and ask them to reflect for a few minutes on a *specific point,* such as "What are the implications of Prospero's decision?" or "How does Mendel's theory fit with what we know about frog reproduction?" And often silence works best, and seals the success of periods of reflection, when we ask students to write something in brief summary or in more length.

Student Journals

There are many ways to use writing to encourage reflection. We will focus on only one here, the journal. Teachers can use journals to encourage more student reflection on classroom ideas and issues. Journals lend themselves to any subject, from marketing to psychology. We will briefly summarize some of the key points for using journals as tools for reflection and urge readers who want a more in-depth analysis to read Fulwiler's *Teaching with Writing* (1987, chap. 2).

The journal begins as a blank notebook in which students write—twice a week at least—some of their thoughts about what they are studying and learning. Fulwiler has his students write their journals while in class; other teachers ask their students to write journal entries at the end of the day or upon returning home or to the dorm. Journal instructions are simple. Students are urged to write down comments on *what they think and feel* about issues, concepts, and events in the day's class, and not to worry too much about grammar and punctuation. As examples, students can write about concerns and frustrations they have experienced with things in class that are unclear to them, they can write about connections they see between a class concept and a newspaper article they read over coffee, or they might reflect in writing on similarities between an issue discussed in class and something they saw on television. In Fulwiler's words, "The journal encourages writers to become conscious, through language, of what is happening to them, both personally and academically" (1987, p. 16).

Though teachers collect, read, and comment on the journals at regular intervals during the quarter (usually three or four times), students are told not to write for the teacher, but to themselves (as in a diary entry or a letter to a friend). The difference between an academic journal and a diary is that the thoughts written down should relate to concepts and issues discussed in the class. Opinion appears split on how to grade journals. Some wisely avoid the issue of assigning a letter grade for a student's personal reflection by using a "full-credit or no-credit" standard. Others use a rating scale: "good insights, adequate, inadequate." Whatever the method, we advise providing some mode of evaluation or credit for journals. Otherwise, they cease to be a priority for students.

Journal writing lets students "step back from an incident, a conversation, a reading, from something heard or seen and reflect upon it with understanding" (Lukinsky, 1990, p. 213). Thus, the journal approach fits neatly with our earlier discussion on reflection as a spur to creating new mental structures. Journals give students time to reflect personally on academic issues and encourage them to see how academic subjects may offer something to their own lives. Teachers also gain a wonderful view of how their students understand what is being taught and how well we are teaching it.

Final Thoughts

In summary, the four elements of active learning—talking and listening, writing, reading, and reflecting—provide building blocks for active-learning strategies. They do so because each element, in its own way, involves a different type of thinking and helps students create new mental structures. We do not fully understand all the intricacies of how these elements work, and we probably never will. What we do know is that if students grapple with subjects through a variety of strategies, they will be more likely to incorporate what they are learning in personally meaningful ways. Now let us look at practical classroom strategies where these elements of active learning can come into play.

THREE

Creating
an Active-Learning
Environment

Using active learning in the classroom requires changes in how we define our roles as teachers. As we suggested earlier, it means spending less time center-stage as a presenter and more time offstage as a designer, choreographer, and manager of the learning environment and teaching process. And how is that accomplished? As this chapter will suggest, teachers need to take time—well before the first class begins—to consider four elements essential to a workable active-learning environment: (1) clarifying course objectives and content, (2) creating a positive classroom tone, (3) coping with teaching space, and (4) knowing more about our students.

Clarifying Course Objectives and Content

Active-learning strategies take time. In a fifty-five-minute classroom session or within the number of class meetings mapped out for a semester, active learning will cut into the time teachers normally spend covering the content they think students need to know. A serious and sometimes perplexing question emerges at this point: Why should teachers give up some of the information about a subject they include in their courses in favor of time for active-learning strategies?

Our initial response to this question is to note that just because teachers may spend less time in class *covering content,* they do not necessarily have to decrease the amount of content *assigned* to students. Still, most practitioners of active learning do decrease the amount of content they require, and we include ourselves in that number. Given the larger philosophical aims of liberal education, we think our time is better spent highlighting issues, focusing student attention on key subject matter, and encouraging discussion, rather than repeating what students can read, for example, in a textbook. Then we are ready to help students learn to use related knowledge and skills in practical ways. In doing all this we have, in fact, begun to redefine "content" to include skills and understanding, as well as information (facts, formulas, terms, names, dates, and so on). As we focus our teaching more on skills and ways of understanding, we discover that it is not necessary to cover as much information as we did in the past. Besides, we know that unless students actually use and appropriate ideas and information, they will not retain them much beyond the conclusion of our courses.

We are not saying that content, as information, is not important. Of course it is. But is it not equally important to teach students how to ask good questions, communicate effectively, critically analyze sources of information, research issues, draw on resources, reflect on consequences, and appreciate diversity? Even if course content is designed for majors, do we want future sociologists and physicists who mostly memorize and recall facts and formulas, or do we want individuals who can solve problems, work cooperatively when necessary, and deal with change? As Richard F. Elmore has stated, "The main value students take away from our classes is not their knowledge of the subject, but a predisposition to learn" (Elmore, 1991, p. xvi). If active learning helps promote this invaluable predisposition to learn, students should be more motivated and more eager to study information we assign, but may not cover in class. In this way, our texts and assigned readings broaden and enhance the key concepts, understandings, and skills we want students to grapple with, rather than simply duplicating what many teachers traditionally include in lectures. But let us return to the real and practical concern of decreasing course content. As a practical matter, we are convinced that in almost every discipline, teachers can winnow content down to the essentials and make room for some experiments with active learning. How is this accomplished?

A good technique is to pose this simple question: "What do I want students *to know* and be able *to do* by the end of this class?" Focusing initially on course outcomes, or the "to do" side of this question, often helps clarify content and appropriate learning strategies. This approach is similar to first deciding what a final exam or final project will be and then considering what students will need to know in order to undertake it successfully. For teachers in disciplines like mathematics, business, and the physical sciences, who normally deal with applications of knowledge, what students are expected *to do* may be fairly self-evident. For teachers in the humanities and social sciences, what it means to do something with the content of a discipline and its information may be less obvious—certainly to the students. However, by concentrating on concrete, practical applications of knowledge, teachers can still get quite specific. Here are some examples:

- *Art history:* "By the end of this course, I want my students prepared to visit an art museum so they can look at a painting and tell me something about its organization in terms of subject matter, composition, perspective, color or medium, and aesthetic qualities."
- *Botany:* "By the end of this course, I want my students able to recognize the central biological processes that make life possible for plants—photosynthesis, respiration, transpiration, reproduction, and so on—and to explain, for example, what such diverse plant communities as those in the Sonoran Desert and the Arctic tundra have in common."
- *Philosophy:* "By the end of this course, I want my students to reflect on aspects of pop culture such as *Rambo*-type movies, self-help articles, and television serials, and to be able to identify and analyze the particular views of human nature portrayed in such media. I expect them to do this analysis in terms of the issues we discussed in class, such as sources of truth, optimism versus pessimism, good versus evil, and nature versus nurture."

Once the "doing" part of a course is a bit more clearly defined, it is relatively easy to backtrack and decide what students need to know in terms of content. The problem is that most of us have unrealistic expectations with regard to what we want students to know. While we may start out with a limited appetite, we usually end up with an overflowing plate of concepts, information, facts, terms—all seemingly essential to our teaching goals. The hard part of our task is deciding what knowledge is "worth having, and hence worth the students' hard work to get and retain" (Charlesworth, 1986, p. 11). Depending on the subject, sorting out what are vital bits of information necessary for students can be a difficult, though always worthwhile, exercise. In some subjects, we may work up a good sweat.

For example, in teaching a typical survey course in economics, how do we decide which information is vital? Obviously, some picking and choosing among several competing aspects of the discipline is necessary. A good textbook and related readings will be essential to give students background information and to acquaint them with methodology, theorists, and issues. In the active-learning classroom, however, economists will have to forsake full textbook coverage in favor of some key concepts, methods, issues, and approaches that are amenable to active-learning strategies. By focusing our time and energy on knowledge critical to understanding our disciplines, we help create a framework for learning that students will embellish with additional information from texts and handouts (Meyers, 1986, p. 54).

Reductions in course content might, however, create problems in sequenced courses in a student's major discipline. To continue with our example, it may be fine to reduce content for students who will take only a survey course in economics, but students majoring in economics need the foundation that teachers in advanced courses will take for granted. If survey courses will cover less content, then departments must agree on how and when to add on what is crucial for advanced courses. This may require developing a transition course, or a crash-course workshop, for students planning to major in economics so that they are prepared for the advanced coursework. Whatever the case, students need to know what we expect of them.

Although it is not a hard-and-fast rule, we think that someone teaching a course in a technical subject, such as human physiology or inorganic chemistry, has less room to maneuver with active-learning strategies than someone teaching a course in humanities, such as American literature or ethics. In certain subjects, like many in the technical-scientific areas, students must gain mastery over specific data and techniques, especially if they are majoring or taking prerequisites for more specialized coursework. The time for extensive active learning in the classroom, then, is necessarily limited. But even here, we believe that a judicious consideration of content will clarify the essential information, concepts, and issues that teachers should emphasize, thus revealing what is less important. Then, by concentrating on essentials, teachers can allow students some time to work with the knowledge they are accumulating.

Once instructors have made decisions about content, the next step is figuring out how to incorporate that content into the larger course objectives. As we have advised, students in an active-learning classroom will not have a steady diet of lectures intended to feed them exactly what we think they need to know. Many students will find this quite a change from what they generally expect from college teaching. Accordingly, they need a concise preview of the course objectives we have in mind at the first class meeting. They also should receive clear information on how class time will be used and class activities will be evaluated. Taking the time necessary in the first class to explain our active-learning approach can "dispel a great deal of anxiety and improve students' disposition toward learning" (Scholl-Buckwald, 1985, p. 18). This change of expectations from the traditional to the active-learning classroom demands a first-rate syllabus.

Typically, a course syllabus includes the outlines of class dates, topics, and reading assignments, as well as the obvious: the official course title and number; prerequisites; your name, office hours, and telephone number; and the required texts and supplies students must purchase. However, a syllabus that will stand up to the demands of active learning needs to be more comprehensive.

We suggest beginning the syllabus with a cover sheet (see Exhibit 3.1) that clearly spells out your expectations for students and their responsibilities in the class. The cover sheet should carry a brief statement explaining what the class is all about in terms of general content, objectives, and outcomes. Next, a section should preview the

Exhibit 3.1. Cover Sheet.

(Phil 340) The Human Condition: A Search for Meaning

Course purpose: The course will explore some of the more problematical and "gutsy" aspects of the human condition using the philosophy of existentialism and examples from literature, plays, and popular media as points of departure. The central organizaing concept for the course is exploring the process of becoming an authentic self. The course will be organized around four primary themes:

> Personal identity and life's meaning
> Freedom and making choices
> Aloneness, loneliness, and solitude
> Death, finitude, and absurdity

An important part of this exploration will involve contrasting the themes above with certain American cultural myths related to freedom, progress, and optimism. In contrast, we will consider some of the central philosophical ideas of three existentialist thinkers: Jean-Paul Sartre, Albert Camus, and Søren Kierkegaard.

Class format: This class differs from more traditional classes in that there will be only brief presentations by the teacher. Classes will focus on round-table discussions of readings. You should come to class prepared to discuss the readings. The seminar will also emphasize a lot of small-group work. Each class will begin with a written problem-solving exercise related to the theme or concept to be discussed in class. Then we will break up into small groups to see how each one of you solved that problem. We will also use small groups during class to raise questions and discuss issues. You will be expected to keep a journal of your thoughts about class discussions. (See handout "Keeping an Academic Journal.") NOTE: Because of this interactive format, your attendance is important. If, for any reason, you miss more than two classes, you will be assigned an additional short paper.

Required reading: The course will use a variety of sources, including Miller's *Death of a Salesman*, Sartre's *No Exit*, selections from Camus's *Myth of Sisyphus* and his *Lyrical Essays*, Kierkegaard's *The Sickness unto Death*, Gilligan's *In a Different Voice*, Sarton's *Journal of a Solitude*, and other brief readings. The main text for the course is Barrett's *Irrational Man*.

Methods of evaluation: In addition to the weekly problem-solving exercises, there will be two required papers. The first paper will be a brief (three- to four-page) paper analyzing the primary themes in *Death of a Salesman*. For the final paper, students will analyze a work of literature in light of the four themes developed in class.

Evaluation Breakdown

Weekly problem-solving exercises	30%	Paper on *Death of a Salesman*	20%
Academic journal	20%	Final analytical paper	30%

Instructor: Chet Meyers
Office hours: MWF, 2–5 p.m. and by appt. 341-7777

types of active-learning strategies (such as small groups and simulations) and course assignments (such as papers and research projects that will be used). Then, students should be informed about how they will be evaluated and how much each evaluation counts overall. Give percentages if you can be so precise. The remainder of the syllabus can focus on classroom dates, topics, reading assignments, study questions, due dates for papers and projects, and additional reminders. Other helpful information might be included as suggested by the syllabus checklist shown in Exhibit 3.2.

One of our colleagues uses an "open letter" approach that accomplishes many of the same things as a cover sheet. After briefly

Exhibit 3.2. Syllabus Checklist.

Consider the following items as a foundation for a syllabus that helps students understand a teacher's expectations as well as basic course information. Including each item may not be necessary. Use this checklist as a guide for what might be included in a course syllabus.

_____ A brief statement of overall course objectives that introduces students to what they should know and be able to do by the end of a course. Consider the personal tone set here as an important aspect of this statement.

_____ A few words about course format, so that students know what to expect about how the teacher will be using class time.

_____ A brief statement of expectations in terms of student responsibilities, clearly stating what the teacher expects (such as participation and the level of work).

_____ A statement of what assessment techniques will be used to evaluate students, including information on grading policies.

_____ A schedule of class dates and topics, along with week-by-week reading assignments.

_____ Due dates for papers, exams, projects, and so on, including any policies about late assignments.

_____ Any pertinent information about academic policies and procedures (such as class attendance, making up assignments, and university-wide policies).

"Nuts-and-bolts" information:

_____ Course title, course number, and prerequisites.

_____ Building and room number.

_____ Instructor's name, phone numbers, and office hours.

_____ Text(s) and supplemental readings.

_____ Suggested bibliography.

---

introducing himself, he distributes his cover letter and his syllabus
and asks students to read through them. He then takes time to
clarify his expectations, emphasizing that in his active-learning
classroom full participation in small-group exercises is important
because lecturing will be held to the minimum. The letter format
this teacher employs lends a nice touch of informality, something
he strives to maintain in his teaching approach, and it helps per-
sonalize the classroom at the outset.

By our taking the time to make a syllabus more explicit and
useful, two important elements of good teaching are emphasized.
First, we clarify in our own minds exactly what we want our students
to learn and how we intend to involve them in learning. Second, we
create a set of clearly marked yardsticks against which students can
measure their progress. Over the years, we have found in our own
classrooms (not surprisingly, of course) that the clearer students are
about what is expected of them, the greater their chances to meet
those expectations.

Creating a Positive Classroom Tone

An active-learning classroom is one that excites students' interests
and encourages their participation. In this regard, how we personally approach a subject makes a difference. The first impression
students draw of us as teachers should be one that conveys both our
enthusiasm for what we are teaching and our confidence in students' learning abilities.

In that context, dressing up a classroom so that it reflects
what is being studied makes good sense. After all, why should the
environment of an anthropology class be the same as that of a math
class? We do not suggest a return to the primary school classroom,
but sometimes a little interior decorating—with charts, maps, pictures, artifacts, posters, signs, and music—can break the ice for
questions and discussions. A zoology professor we know routinely
brings in animals (stuffed and alive) that help to start discussions
in several of his classes. A history professor sets the tone of each class
period with recordings of music and posters contemporary to the
eras his students will be studying.

If you teach in a room of your own or share a classroom with a colleague from the same discipline, improving the physical environment is a bit easier than if you are a nomad. Still, the Bedouins prove very adept at carrying their means of livelihood around with them. Newspapers, magazines, posters, and other objets d'art may seem a burden to lug around, but students do notice and appreciate these attempts to enliven our teaching.

Taking time to create an interesting physical environment can have the added benefit of settling students down and focusing them on the tasks at hand. Think back to your own student days and consider all the things buzzing around in your brain as you rushed to class: an upcoming exam in another course, getting your clothes to the laundromat, the Homecoming Weekend . . . . Suffice it to say, it took a while to focus in on the anthropology professor's lecture on the fishing rituals of the Trobriand Islanders. If we accept that initially most students' minds are not centered on what we have in store for the day's class, and if we want them to be more involved in their own learning, then it makes sense to give them some time to settle in before the class starts.

Some teachers simply ask students to sit quietly for a minute or two, relax, and center-in by reflecting about one question they may have had from the last class. Others use the first ten minutes of the class period to warm up students with an active-learning exercise. As Kenneth Eble advised: "Whatever a teacher can do to provide an easy transition from the student's real world to the artificial world of the classroom is likely to be appreciated and to aid learning" (Eble, 1988, p. 34). For example, a short news article, a feature story, a photo, artwork, an artifact, a cartoon, or a film clip could serve as a focal point for a brief problem-solving discussion. Such an exercise helps students relax, look ahead to the day's subject, and participate from the start.

Whatever you choose to do, figure out some way to put your students in the right mood to concentrate, free from outside distractions and ready to participate in the day's activities.

Another important aspect in establishing an active-learning tone is our own presence as teachers. We probably convey as much to students nonverbally as we do through our words. Students quickly sense if a teacher respects their contributions to class or if, indeed, the teacher wants contributions at all. If we do not believe

Teaching Tip: Focusing Students

Earl Bolick, a professor of management, begins his three-hour classes with a videotape entitled "Classical Images: A Concert in Nature." There is no dialogue, simply scenes from nature backed up with classical music. The tape is running as students arrive in class. Previously, Bolick has informed students to close their books when they arrive, sit back, and focus on the video monitor. He tells them he will "blink" the lights once, a minute before turning the tape off. As Bolick says, "The charm of creation and the calming sound of music help sweep aside the many conflicts, anxieties, and distractions students bring with them to the classroom." And it works. Recently, during the fourth week of a quarter, Bolick forgot to bring the tape and large numbers of students complained. According to Bolick, students are ready to learn when the tape goes off and the class begins. Some students even show up early for class just to relax.

in students' abilities to contribute, they will quickly get the message. Think back to the teachers you had. Which ones do you remember and why? Did that inspiring math teacher you remember so fondly stand up and declare: "I really love this subject, and I want you to enjoy it with me!" Probably not, but after a few classes you got her message. And what about that stodgy literature teacher who made you feel just a little further down the evolutionary scale than a slime mold? He probably never said as much. But as he peered over his glasses at you with undisguised intellectual superiority, you got the message. It goes without saying that our academic body language says volumes about us as teachers.

During that first class, students will read us to see how we expect them to behave, and to see if we really want them to participate. Not long ago, a faculty member participating in Metropolitan State's University's teaching-improvement program asked for a videotape of his class. He thought, perhaps, that a videotape might reveal why his students never seemed to respond when he asked for their questions. To his chagrin, it did! At one point in the tape, a student in the first row asked an obvious question about the syllabus. The teacher winced as the camera recorded him turning away from the student with a disappointed look on his face and responding curtly to the question. "No wonder they never ask questions," he confessed to a colleague watching the tape with him. "I killed that possibility the first day of class!"

Knowing that students pick up on both our verbal and nonverbal messages can guide us in creating a positive active-learning environment. For example, it is a good idea to be in the classroom before the students arrive, especially the first day of class. Being in the classroom as students come in shows that we care about teaching and learning. It also lets our students know that we are anxious to meet them and to get things started with a minimum of delay and confusion. In subsequent class periods throughout the term, this before-class time can be used to talk with students informally and to answer quick questions. Some teachers regularly employ this informal talking time as a transition to their day's presentation. They find that it allows students to decompress and shift gears from the previous class or other concerns. Thus, the students are more prepared to deal with what the class will cover that day.

There are many ways to personally communicate a positive classroom tone, and the small investment in time we make for our students will benefit all concerned. However, for students accustomed to the traditional classroom, in which teachers are active and students accept their role as passive receptors, the shift to active learning requires a clear message from teachers that those old rules have changed and new expectations are in order. How we organize the actual environment and physical space of a classroom is a big part of that message.

Coping with Teaching Space

In many instances—especially for untenured faculty at large universities—teachers have little to say about where they teach. At smaller schools, however, it may be possible to have some influence in securing a classroom that is amenable to active learning. If this is the case for you, take the initiative, do some reconnoitering, and make your desires known before the scheduling office puts your class in the World War II quonset hut next to the experimental hybrid-corn patch.

For many of us, the best imaginable active-learning classroom would be large enough to easily seat about twenty-five students in comfortable, movable desks or swivel chairs that can be arranged in a U-shape (Welty, 1989), a circle, and smaller groupings. The ideal classroom also would have all the accoutrements: good lighting, ventilation, and acoustics; overhead projectors and media-communications equipment galore; and plenty of blackboard or poster space.

Too often, however, perfection remains an elusive ideal, and the reality of available classroom sites proves to be a sobering experience. As we all recognize, the architects of higher education generally have favored either the narrow, shoe-box classroom or its big brother, the giant lecture hall. Both usually are supplied with an assortment of desks or chairs, bolted to the floor. The vastness of the lecture hall isolates students from each other and from their teachers, while the cramped shoe box creates a claustrophobic and sometimes chaotic atmosphere that is hardly conducive to learning. In both cases, fixed classroom furniture better serves a janitor's penchant for tidiness than an educator's need for flexibility.

The design and arrangement of teaching space says volumes about a college or university's philosophy of education, and in most cases, that message does not encourage active learning. Until quality teaching space becomes a priority, most of us are faced with three basic teaching situations: (1) adequately sized rooms with flexible seating for small classes, (2) large lecture halls with permanent or inflexible seating, or (3) small, crowded classrooms with little room for movement.

What follows are some suggestions for taking best advantage of whatever space we find ourselves teaching in.

Adequate Space

If you are scheduled to teach in a room with either movable desks or tables, take advantage of this flexibility to create some good active-learning arrangements. Here are a few examples.

The U-shape. This configuration is highly recommended by Minnesota Mining and Manufacturing Company (3M) from its research with the Wharton School of Business on promoting successful meetings. This arrangement makes it easy to see all students, promotes interchanges around and across the table, and gives students a clear view of any overhead, blackboard, or video-slide-movie presentations. As pictured in Figure 3.1, students sit around the outside of a U-shaped configuration of tables. The teacher sits or stands at the open end.

Figure 3.1. The U-Shape.

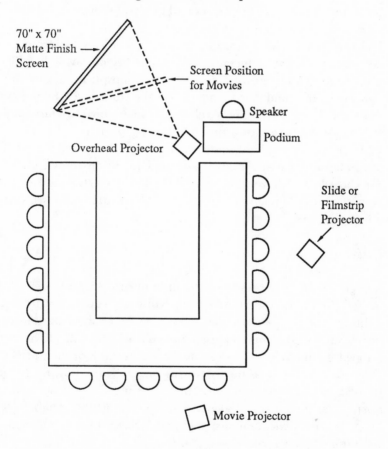

Source: *How to Run Better Business Meetings,* 1987, p. 67. Used by permission.

According to 3M, this configuration is good both for smaller classes of ten to fifteen students and for those of twenty to twenty-five students. It avoids the "empty feeling found in most large rooms" (*How to Run Better Business Meetings,* 1987). The U-shape allows students to see each other and encourages discussion. It also helps teachers see each student clearly, talk with them directly, and make a quick dash to a nearby blackboard to write down important points. Teachers can and should move around freely, as nothing is gained in an active-learning classroom by standing immobile behind a lectern. This arrangement also allows students to move their tables and chairs apart and into small groups for discussion.

The Circle. A circle of desks or chairs works nicely for groups of twenty to twenty-five students where tables are not available. The advantages include creating an inclusive atmosphere that encourages interaction and discussion among the students by taking the focus off the teacher. The circle also can be broken into small groups for discussion and problem-solving purposes. (See Figure 3.2.) The circle does have some disadvantages, however. For example, you cannot easily roam about and jot things down on the blackboard. And if you are using overhead projectors and media presentations, a circle must be rearranged for students to see what is being presented.

Large, Impersonal Space

A large lecture room presents difficult problems. Students are seated in ascending rows from front to back. Noise echoes cavernously, and lighting is often more suitable to a romantic evening than to learning chemistry. Students feel disconnected from each other. They are trapped in an environment that makes them think of their teacher as an entertainer and themselves as an audience waiting to be pleased. Asking a question or participating in a dialogue with their teacher can give many students a severe case of stage fright. The large classroom encourages silence and makes all but the most adventurous students passive spectators.

If the classroom is huge and the number of students is small, a more intimate environment can be created by grouping students

Figure 3.2. The Circle.

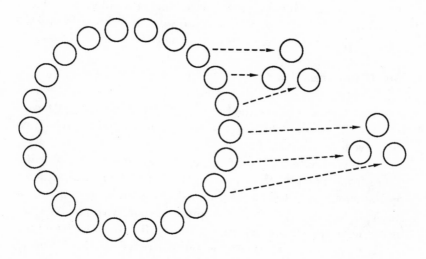

toward the front of the room. If chairs and desks can be moved easily, we can make a smaller "room" for our students. Or, if the desks are permanently bolted in place, we can use a portion of the large room.

But what about those huge survey courses with a student cast of hundreds? Can these situations be made more intimate for learning? Well, one of our colleagues, teaching a large survey course in psychology, assigns each of her students to a small work group (containing six students) and structures assignments so that the work groups meet once a week outside of class. Sometimes the assignments focus on simply clarifying reading assignments (for this she uses study questions). At other times, the work groups deal with a problem related to the week's topic. If you have the luxury of working with good teaching assistants, why not assign them to monitor and help out with small groups? If not, these groups can work amazingly well on their own if they are given a few guidelines for interaction (see Chapter Four for examples).

Within the large lecture class itself, it is possible—though a bit noisy—to engage in a number of active-learning strategies (Frederick, 1987b). We will explore these in the following chapters. But to give you the flavor, will tell you what one of our colleagues does in his accounting lectures. At least twice a week, during his fifty-minute classes, he breaks students into pairs or small groups of four to raise questions, discuss issues, or solve problems. Figure 3.3 shows how such arrangements can be made.

Small, Cramped Space

If your classroom is designed for twenty students and you have a class of thirty, some daunting physical and psychological barriers to active learning stand in your way.

We all have a sense of our own space and comfortable distance from others. If that space is compressed, students naturally grow more concerned about personal boundaries than about the topic for the day. Such an environment is hardly conducive to an active-learning classroom. Recall how difficult it was to learn pressed up against a wall and gagging for fresh air in the stuffy, overheated classrooms of "Old Main." A cramped space also means that students might not have good sight lines for overhead projections, blackboards, and audiovisual presentations. Good eye contact between students and teachers is next to impossible.

What can we do? It would be foolish to suggest that there are any easy answers to dealing with overcrowded teaching spaces. Because a small, cramped space inhibits student interaction, think of ways to move some groups out of the classroom, perhaps into the hall or a nearby room that is empty. If it seems appropriate, move the entire class to a new location. Consider a visit to the library to explore basic research techniques or plan a trip to a community event related to your subject. One of our colleagues suggest splitting the class in half on some occasions. If class sessions are longer than fifty minutes—say ninety minutes or three hours—we can schedule a few meetings so that part of the class shows up for the first half of the normal meeting time and others meet in the remaining half. Review sessions are a perfect time to schedule split sessions. Students have more of an opportunity to participate, and those having trouble with the course can get more attention. So, for example, students having trouble mastering basic concepts might meet with the teacher during the first half, while students at a more advanced level can voice their concerns during the second half of the session.

Figure 3.3. Grouping Students in a Lecture Hall.

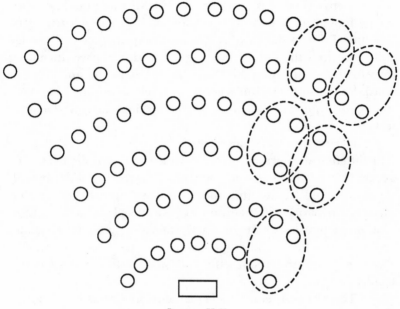

Lecture Hall

Source: Meyers, 1986, p. 66. Reprinted by permission.

Naturally, teachers need to take care in proposing these choices so as not to unfairly brand some students as the "smart ones" and others as the "dumb ones." During these less crowded split sessions, teachers can ask about specific concerns that might not come up when students are packed together like sardines.

Another solution for crowded classes is to divide the students into ongoing small work groups (as we suggested in the previous section on large classes) that report back to the larger group on their activities. Finally, if a pinched classroom space is a chronic problem at your school—organize! Get together with some kindred spirits and form a faculty classroom committee. Draw up a list of guidelines on classroom space and make recommendations to administrators, preceded perhaps by having them attend a class session to get a firsthand "environmental impact statement."

We know from our own struggles, at a university that prides itself on small classes and adequate space, that the battle for a good teaching environment is ongoing. In 1990, Metropolitan State University moved its Minneapolis classrooms into a newly renovated building. Prior to the move, a faculty committee met with the architect to stress the importance of good teaching space, including carpeted floors and movable tables and chairs. The architect listened. So far, so good. But when the movers set up the new classrooms, they put all the tables and chairs in neat rows facing a lectern.

During the next quarter, teachers were urged to experiment with different arrangements for tables and chairs in order to encourage an interactive classroom. Some faculty stood in solidarity with the movers and left the furniture as it was originally set up, but many faculty broke with tradition and rearranged the narrow, eight-foot-long tables and chairs into new, interactive designs. To get an idea of how a little creativity can alter the classroom atmosphere, compare the original room setup with some of the alternatives our faculty designed (Figure 3.4).

The physical setup of a classroom does say a lot to students about the patterns of interaction we expect from them. When all students see of their classmates is the back of their heads, and all eyes are directed to the teacher at the front of the room, a not-too-subtle message is delivered as to what is really important. No matter what we *say* about wanting students to be more responsible for their learning, the physical and psychological environment of a classroom speaks with more authority. In this context, ill-fitting classrooms can frustrate the best of active-learning strategies. However, with a little imagination, we can still make the best of a bad deal.

Knowing More About Our Students

To practice active learning successfully, we should know something about each of our students, and particularly what they think and feel about the specific subjects we teach. While this sounds like common sense, surprisingly few teachers use information about their students' backgrounds, interests, knowledge, and attitudes to the best advantage. All of this personal information can be translated into active teaching and learning that takes individual differences and levels of experience into account. In short, we need to know a little about who our students are and what they know. After all, some students (especially adults) may know more about a given topic than we do.

One way to efficiently identify information about students is through a brief survey form. Developing a survey form does not take much time, and it can prove invaluable by alerting us to any unique knowledge and experiences students can contribute. Gathering this kind of information lets students know that we take them seriously and want to learn from them as well. In the first class, a survey form can be handed out, completed, and collected in ten to fifteen minutes. Before distributing the survey, tell the students how the information will be used, so they will consider the exercise worthwhile. Survey findings then can be tabulated quickly and the results shared with students at the next class.

Student surveys can be used for a variety of purposes. Three particular tasks come to mind: (1) uncovering student attitudes and predispositions toward our discipline, (2) finding out about students' general or specific areas of interest, and (3) getting a reading on students' present skills and knowledge in a given area.

Student Attitudes and Predispositions

One of our colleagues begins his introductory philosophy classes by asking students to draw an image that comes to mind when they think of a philosopher. Not surprisingly, the images are depressingly similar: our colleague reports, "Students usually envision an old man, with a beard and long, unruly hair, tweed coat, smoking a pipe, and (this really hurts) spouting irrelevancies." This particular teacher knows from the first class that he has some powerful attitudinal barriers to overcome. By bringing to the surface negative stereotypes, faulty perceptions, and downright hostility, we can acknowledge problems and misconceptions, address them directly, and start to reverse negative attitudes that often impede learning.

Student Interests

A survey can provide valuable information about topics and issues that already interest students. Often, this knowledge can be used for

Figure 3.4. Alternative Room Arrangements.

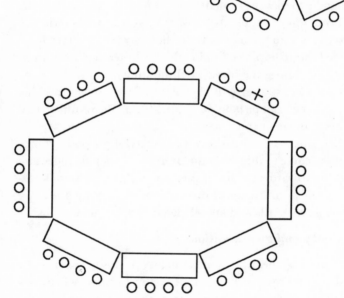

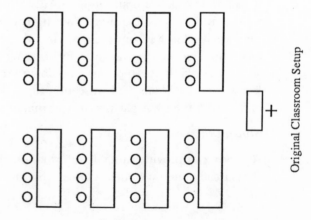

Original Classroom Setup

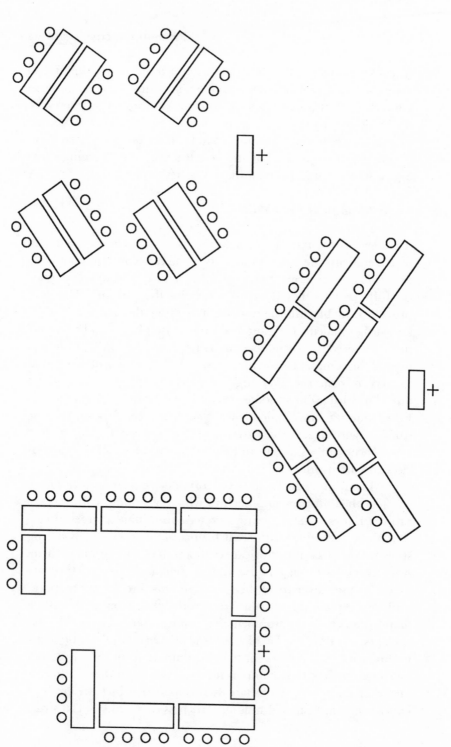

special assignments, discussion, and extra projects. We might find a number of students interested in the same things. For example, in a modern social-problems class, students indicating an interest in the homeless might develop a cooperative final project. Obviously, in this situation, opportunities abound to encourage students' interests, since we know that the best teaching and learning often begins with what is most familiar to students.

Student Knowledge and Skills

A survey of this nature can take the form of a simple pretest in which students are asked to identify some concepts and issues and to define certain terms. Surveys of this nature need to be designed carefully so that they do not overwhelm the students. They can provide valuable information by indicating the general level of knowledge students have attained in our disciplines and how much time we need to spend on fundamentals. Obviously, teaching beyond the comprehension of students can be a source of frustration to everyone concerned. We might also discover that our students are quite knowledgeable in some areas. It does not make much sense to waste time teaching in depth what students already know. Those students with a good background in coursework and some solid experience with a subject can help others in the small-group exercises and discussions (see Exhibit 3.3).

If putting together a survey form does not strike your fancy, consider the following approach in which one of our colleagues, a historian, uses a simple writing exercise to initiate a larger discussion about the value of different historical perspectives. By asking students to focus on a historical event personally important to them, Anne Webb opens the door for all her students to share perspectives that reflect the diversity of their backgrounds. Providing an opportunity to express this diversity makes the classroom potentially a more comfortable environment for women and culturally diverse students. On the first day of class, she asks her social-history class to think of a historical event that was important in their lives and asks them to describe its importance and effects on them. Students then exchange papers and share their responses, which are grouped under common historical headings, such as economics, social struc-

Exhibit 3.3. First-Day Survey.

Statistics 1 (Bob Raymond, Professor)

Please give me some information about yourself. I will use this information to adapt this course more precisely to each student's needs. Please use the back of this form and the extra sheet to write your responses to the following:

1. Tell me about any experience you've had with statistics (courses, employment, family business, and so on).
2. What do you think of when you hear the word *statistics*?
3. What do you think this course will be like?
4. Do you have any worries about being successful in this course?
5. How do you think statistics relates to your career goals?
6. If you have used a computer:
   a. How much experience do you have?
   b. What kinds of computers have you used?
   c. What functions did you perform with a computer?
7. Do you have a calculator that can give square roots?
8. Although this is not a math course, sometimes math skills are needed. For each of the topics below, check the appropriate column.

I Need Review   I'm Comfortable with This Topic

Absolute value
Square root
Notation for sums (sigma)
Graphs
Idea of probability
Fractions
Percentages

---

ture, politics, and culture. This exercise shows how history can be divided into categories and how those categories often overlap. Webb then pushes students to consider other areas of historical experience that have strongly influenced their lives, such as religion, feminism, or multicultural viewpoints. In doing so, she leads students to discuss the importance of religion, gender, and multicultural perspectives for appreciating the past, to speculate on why they have been ignored in historical study, and to consider how historians disagree about the basic, driving forces of historical development.

Finding out something about students is important, but we

also encourage teachers to tell students something about their own interests and backgrounds. A few minutes during the first class can be used to describe how we first got interested in our discipline and why we find it so fascinating. Students also like to hear about some of our outside interests and avocational pursuits. All of this can help make the teaching enterprise more human and break down artificial barriers. Of course, talking personally and informally with students is a matter of individual taste; it should not be forced or exaggerated. As with all the strategies and teaching tips in this book, we suggest that teachers only try out what they feel comfortable with.

Final Thoughts

In an active-learning classroom, teachers no longer control students' learning by exercising power from the front of the room and depending primarily on transmitting knowledge through lectures. Instead, they direct and choreograph what happens in a classroom so that students can begin taking responsibility for their learning. The direction and choreography of students engaged in "doing" science, anthropology, or mathematics will benefit a great deal from planning and groundwork undertaken by teachers before the first class period. To get things started right, teachers must figure out what students need "to know and to do"; write a syllabus that clearly outlines course objectives, expectations, and methods of learning; create a classroom environment that supports and enlivens student participation in learning; deal creatively with the realities of assigned teaching space; and find out more about students' interests, lives, experiences, and capabilities. If we do all this, we have a much better chance of contributing to our students' growth as liberally educated citizens and of increasing our own enjoyment of teaching.

PART 2

Strategies
and Techniques

FOUR

Informal
Small Groups

Designing informal small-group activities is a relatively easy way to begin creating an active-learning classroom. Small groups can be just the right ticket for many active-learning tasks, such as lecture summaries, clarification of reading assignments, and problem solving. But there is nothing magical about putting students together in groups. Small-group activities are educationally sound only insofar as we carefully design realistic goals, guide students' behavior, and create a positive atmosphere in which students will share their ideas and learn from each other.

So before rushing to adopt small-group activities, we need to pause and reflect on what makes small groups an effective teaching and learning strategy. Here we should consider what happens in small groups and what teachers can do to provide students with guidelines for positive interaction. While one need not be an expert in group dynamics to use small groups, some basic considerations are essential for positive results.

What Happens in Small Groups

Turning students loose in small groups means letting go of the typical classroom power structure and the comfort it affords us as teachers. As we suggested earlier, active learning only succeeds to the degree that we are willing to step out of the teaching spotlight and let our students assume more responsibility for their own learning. Most of us will approach this situation with some initial misgivings. We should be assured, though, by the observations of some respected educators, that wonderful things can happen when students work together in small groups, provided we have carefully structured those interactions and built in key elements of active learning.

One of the primary strengths of small-group activities is that they can incorporate all the key elements of active learning—talking and listening, reading, writing, and reflecting. They also help students learn important interpersonal skills. Let us briefly consider how these elements and skills can be integrated in small-group activities.

As we suggested in Chapter Two, a simple yet powerful process of clarification occurs in talking things out. By clarifying and testing their own ideas and perceptions in small-group discussions, students expand their thinking abilities in ways even the best teachers cannot achieve through traditional approaches. The best small-group activities are those in which everyone gets a chance to voice their perspective on an issue or problem. Three aspects of active learning occur in this context: the process of *talking* helps the speakers clarify their thoughts, while those *listening* get the opportunity to *reflect* on alternatives to their own perspectives.

Peers often have a legitimacy that superiors lack. Students will listen to things from each other they will not accept from teachers. Piaget suggested that the "social transmission" of knowledge, which takes place when children interact with each other and test their ideas against those of their peers, is one of the most powerful forces in expanding students' thinking abilities (Ginsberg and Oper, 1969, pp. 169–170). By carefully structuring student interactions in small groups, teachers promote what developmental experts have dubbed "higher-order reasoning"—in other words, analyzing, evaluating, and critiquing abilities. Once again, Wulff, Nyquist, and Abbott's three-year study of students' learning in large classes is instructive. They found "that the second most frequently mentioned dimension that assisted students in learning in large classes was other students. Such a finding suggests that large class instructors may want to think about ways to capitalize on collaboration possibilities in the large class context" (1987, p. 29). But having students talk with each other is not in itself adequate as a strategy for clarification. Often students remain confused about central concepts, issues, and theories. Most teachers who use small groups have students report back their findings to the large class so the teachers can clarify areas of confusion and misinterpretation.

When small-group activities combine *reading* and *writing* with talking and listening, two additional skills that help clarify thinking abilities come into play. Teachers often use short pieces of reading to initiate small-group activities. For example, an economics professor hands out an editorial from yesterday's paper that discusses dropping interest rates and their effect on housing starts. This relates to a discussion in the previous class about antirecessionary policies. Reading such an editorial requires students to see connections and to sort through information in order to draw their own conclusions. Once they have had the opportunity to read through the editorial, the teacher may ask them to write down their thoughts before talking with classmates about their ideas.

Though we do not know exactly what happens when we put pen to paper, we do know that something important takes place. According to writing expert Toby Fulwiler: "The more people write, the better they learn; writing is the most powerful use of language for developing sustained critical thought; it helps people to visualize thought and therefore to modify, extend, develop or criticize it" (McNeil, 1988, p. 88).

Starting group activities with individual writing has additional benefits as well. The quiet time that writing requires encourages participation of those students whose learning style is more reflective and who take a little longer before their brain engages with their mouth. As Garrison Keillor might observe, shy people need more time to compose themselves.

A final, important outcome of small-group activity is the development of social and interpersonal skills students achieve through interacting with each other. But these skills do not materialize from the ether. Students must be guided in their interactions. With proper guidance, they can learn valuable skills to serve them outside the classroom. They will learn:

- To be good listeners
- To cooperate in a common task
- To give and receive constructive feedback

- To respect differences of opinion
- To support their judgments with evidence
- To appreciate diverse points of view (gender, culture, and so on)

With all these potential outcomes at our command, it is doubly important to be clear about the purposes we want small groups to accomplish.

The Purpose of Small Groups

The clearest advantage group activities afford over traditional teaching is the opportunity for larger numbers of students to voice their ideas. Students who might never speak in a large-classroom setting will participate in small groups. In so doing, they will gain confidence in their own learning abilities and the worthiness of their ideas. Of course, the types of skills students develop will depend on the objectives teachers want to accomplish.

A wide variety of small-group activities can be used to engage our students. These activities range from what David and Roger Johnson and Edythe Johnson Holubec (1990) call *informal small groups* (for example, simply pairing students off to share questions about a given topic) to more complex efforts that we refer to as *cooperative student projects* (for example, having five students serve as an ongoing, peer feedback group offering comments, critiques, and suggestions for improving student papers). Although informal small groups and cooperative projects share common elements of active learning, we make a distinction between the two. As we see it, informal small groups are typically short-term and can be used in simple tasks such as summarizing main points in a lecture or uncovering student concerns. The investment students have in informal small groups is immediate and short-term. Thus, these groups can change from class to class or even in the same class period. Cooperative projects, on the other hand, involve students in longer-term commitments, such as an entire semester, and may result in a group project that receives a common grade. They might even entail the formation of a study group that meets regularly outside the class. In these situations, students have more investment in the group's success, because they must rely on each other for long-term assistance in mastering the subject matter.

In this chapter, we will emphasize easily adaptable informal group activities because they are a natural starting point for those of us who are ready to get our feet wet using small groups. We will save the plunge into cooperative projects until Chapter Five.

Informal small groups are simple to design, involve relatively low risk, and pay big dividends in terms of allowing students to apply and adopt personally what we are trying to teach. Some professors like to start each class by grouping students in threes or fours and giving them a specific task, such as "Summarize as best you can the main points in the chapter on plate tectonics." Others may ask rhetorical questions that will get students' minds percolating before a lecture, such as "If B. F. Skinner's view of human nature is correct, what does that say about how we treat criminals in our state prison?" Usually, five minutes is sufficient time to get small groups working on such problems. A benefit of these activities is that they help settle students down for the day's work. At the end of a class, small groups can be used to summarize issues and concerns. Giving students time at the end of class to reflect and to clarify new learning through small groups helps ensure that they are doing more than just taking notes.

In the teaching model that concludes this chapter, we have highlighted a well-constructed group exercise that offers some hints teachers may want to adopt in their classes. Before we present that teaching model, however, let us summarize some of the *objectives* of informal small groups that might fit any class, regardless of size. Small groups, for example, can be used to:

- *Generate* ideas in preparation for a lecture, film, and so on
- *Summarize* main points in a text, reading, film, or lecture
- *Assess* levels of skills and understanding
- *Reexamine* ideas presented in previous classes
- *Review* exams, problems, quizzes, and writing assignments
- *Process* learning outcomes at the end of class
- *Provide* comments to teachers on how a class is going
- *Compare and contrast* key theories, issues, and interpretations

- *Solve* problems that relate theory to practice
- *Brainstorm* applications of theory to everyday life

Of course, a small-group activity might accomplish more than one of these objectives. However, delimiting objectives is wise, as students usually can focus on only one or two outcomes. Whatever purposes we choose, being clear about our instructional objectives for any small-group activity is crucial to its success. For example, in an introductory philosophy class, Larry Crockett uses a small-group exercise to prepare students for the day's lecture. He puts students into groups of four and gives them a few questions based on the assigned readings for that class and focused on materials he hopes to cover. The students work on these questions in small groups at the beginning of class and then feed their responses back to the larger group. Crockett uses these responses as a lead-in to his lecture for the day. As a result, students are less hesitant to interrupt; they ask questions and make comments. Crockett reports that what used to be a monologue has changed to a meaningful dialogue.

The primary objective of the preceding example is that of preparation—plowing the field, so to speak, so that students are ready to receive the seed. Such an objective is quite different from that of a small-group exercise intended to compare and contrast theories presented in the previous class. However we decide to use small groups, our original intent is the key, because it helps determine how we will size up these groups and what kind of operating guidelines we will give our students.

> *But do small groups work?* Yes! In a comparative study of students in separate classes of introductory statistics, C. Robert Borreson discovered that students who worked in small groups on statistical assignments scored significantly better (in terms of final grade points) than did students working individually in another class, studying the same course content [Borreson, 1990].

Structuring Groups for Success

Group size can vary according to our objectives. If a lot of interchange is our goal, and we just want to start a class discussion, then pairing students or creating groups of three ensures an animated dialogue. Groups this size are good for generating ideas, summarizing the week's readings, and reviewing the main points of a day's work. However, for problem-solving tasks, larger groups of four to six work best. In groups larger than six, passive students find it easier to remain silent and the groups lose their overall advantages. A colleague, Linda Scott, restricts her groups to four and begins group exercises with students working first in pairs. She reminds us with infallible logic: "It's hard to get left out of a pair."

Small groups can be formed as casually as having students turn to the person beside them and work in pairs. Or, for larger groups, we can draw a lesson from our junior high physical education classes and number-off. In classes where student seating varies with each class session, small groups usually assume a different mix each time we form them. In these situations, students are exposed to a variety of perspectives on issues as the composition of the groups change. However, if students are assigned regular seats or choose to sit in the same seats for each class, then some attention should be paid to the gender, age, and cultural composition of the groups.

The dynamics of small groups are such that, in most cases, those in the minority will prefer silence to active participation. For example, one man in a group of four women students might be as hesitant to speak as might a woman if the situation were reversed. The same consideration holds true for students from different cultures. If, for example, you have only two African American students in your class, you may feel that you are being egalitarian by placing them in two separate small groups, yet they may feel more at ease working in the same small group. Get to know your students individually as soon as possible, and then plan your small groups with a sensible, pragmatic approach. Without making a big to-do about these issues, we should take care that small groups have the best *working* balance—even if this might mean that one group is composed mostly of women and another of all Latino students.

Whatever works best toward the goal of active participation by students is what makes sense!

How well small groups operate depends on the clarity of their objectives (Why are we doing this exercise?), the parameters of the activity (What exactly are we to do?), and the guidelines agreed upon for interaction (How should we behave?). Students quickly figure out if time spent in small groups is worthwhile or ready-made for goofing off. Teachers cannot assume that students know how to behave in small groups. We have to guide their positive interactions. Some teachers go as far as modeling small-group activities on the first day of class so that students can see how a good small group works. Other teachers distribute small-group guidelines (see the suggestions later in this section) and take time to make sure that the students understand them. Once small groups are operating, it makes good sense for teachers to roam around—as unobtrusively as possible—to see how things are working. By gently intervening when we see problems, such as one student dominating a group, we can usually nip these bad habits in the bud. It will not be long before the groups operate pretty much on their own steam.

Teaching Tip: Small-Group Icebreaker

Judith Litterst, a speech-communications teacher, reminds us that faculty should borrow a tip from small-group theory on "primary tension," the initial unease people feel in small groups. The first meeting of a group can be slow starting since people are unfamiliar with each other and with the task they are assigned. Allow for some get-acquainted time and don't be too anxious to move quickly into discussion. Let folks briefly introduce themselves to the group, perhaps by telling others what they hope to learn in the course and how it might apply to their everyday lives.

For those of us new at using small groups, it makes sense to start with a rather simple format. For example, what about asking students to pair off and discuss what they thought the main point was in that handout covering the prenuptial rites of mountain gorillas. The guidelines for such an exercise can be simple. First, instruct the pairs to take three minutes for each person to summarize what the reading assignment covered. Then, the pairs should spend another three minutes coming to some agreements about the main points in the reading. The teacher's role is to act as a timekeeper. A flip of the light switch at each three-minute interval will move students on to the next task.

Behavior guidelines for such an exercise are simple. When one student talks, the other listens. Questions of clarification are okay, but no critiquing is permitted during the initial sharing. Achieving consensus naturally will involve some negotiation. Once the pairs have finished their work, it is time to call on a few students to see what they learned from the assigned reading.

Students can learn much from a simple exercise like this. They learn to formulate their own ideas and back them up with evidence. They learn to listen carefully to another's point of view. They learn to negotiate a consensus. And—we really like this one— they learn to do each week's reading before coming to class. Teachers also learn. They receive answers to the questions, Did the reading accomplish what we intended? Did it lend easily to good discussions? Are students really doing their homework?

As small-group activities grow more complex, guidelines must be more precise and structured. For example, in groups of four to six, a few students may be assigned specific roles. Role assignments depend on the nature of the activity. If students are asked to brainstorm a list of resources concerning ground-water pollution, we may only want to assign a "recorder" to write down ideas from the group's discussion and an "encourager" to make sure everyone contributes. If the group activity involves more sophisticated problem solving, the roles of "clarifier" (one who makes sure that the group understands what each person is proposing) and "mediator" (one who helps the group arrive at a consensus) can be added. In *Circles of Learning* (1990), Johnson, Johnson, and Johnson Holubec suggest a number of different roles students can play in small-group activities.

No matter what goal is intended for an activity, we urge the preparation of a written handout that tells students *why* they are in small groups, *what* they are expected to do, and *how* they should act in the group situation. Since students do not come to class as natural collaborators, a clear set of guidelines on the subject can save a lot of pain and anxiety. As a start, here are some instructions you might include in any list of small-group guidelines:

- *Silence is okay.* Think before speaking.
- *Stick with assigned roles.* If the teacher has assigned specific roles for the group, agree on who's who and do not switch.
- *If you do not understand what another person has said, ask for clarification.*
- *Respect the contributions of others.* One of the purposes of small-group activity is to learn to see things from perspectives different from your own.
- *Do not dominate the discussion and do not interrupt while a classmate is speaking.* Try to give "equal air time" for everyone in the group.

More extended guidelines are in order for small-group activities that ask students to complete rather sophisticated tasks. In those cases, group members must learn how to depend on each other, how to hold each other accountable for individual responsibility, and how to assess their group's progress. At this stage, however, we have moved from *informal* group work to what we have labeled *cooperative student projects.* And that's a subject we will cover in our next chapter.

Managing the Classroom for Small Groups

Once groups are formed, our role switches from design and architectural consultant to time manager or "whistle blower." When students get into small-group activity, they become quite animated and classroom noise levels skyrocket. Inevitably, the time comes when enthusiasm must be interrupted in order to reconvene the class and discuss outcomes. At times like this you almost need a fire alarm to get the students' attention because their discussions are so spirited. In fact, students get so wound up in their discussions that calling them back to order seems almost criminal. But do not feel guilty. Even though we must intervene and interrupt what a col-

Teaching Tip: Disagreeing Without Put-Downs

Whenever students must reach a small-group decision, some degree of controversy is inevitable. Linda Scott sees this controversy as an opportunity, not a problem. With our help, Scott suggests, students can learn to view controversy as a *mutual* problem, rather than as a competitive win-lose situation. Often, when someone disagrees with us, we tend to take it personally and see it as a threat to our self-esteem. However, students can learn to use controversy as an opportunity to clarify group discussion, encourage the participation of others, and, in so doing, generate a better overall response to the question or issue under discussion.

To help students reframe disagreement in a positive context, Scott asks students to think of specific, nonthreatening things they can say to each other—in other words, helpful forms of disagreeing. She also solicits specific examples of disagreements that are sure to put down the other person. She writes both kinds of responses on the board, constructing what she calls a T-chart. This chart can then be copied and given to students for future reference at the next class meeting.

Say this:	*Instead of this:*
I don't think I agree. Could you explain?	That doesn't make sense at all.
I disagree because . . . or, I see it differently because . . .	Wow! Is that ever dumb.
I think we should check our notes and the original assignment.	That's not what the teacher asked us to do.
It might be better to . . .	You are dead wrong

Have you considered . . . ? Could it also be . . .	
Does everyone agree?	Let's vote on it.
I understand how you feel, but I think you might consider . . .	That really offends me!
Act like this:	*Instead of this:*
Pleasant, relaxed, normal tones of voice.	An "attack posture," angry or disinterested facial expressions, loud or strident voice.

league calls "the teachable moment," it is a necessary break. Better to stop them while they are churning than wait until groups are finished and the room assumes that uncomfortable silence we all know too well.

Another important role we play in managing small groups is that of "intervention specialist." It would be wonderful if students always followed our guidelines and their discussions were enthusiastic and respectful. And most times they do quite well. But we have all had encounters with certain students who just do not seem to catch on. Prime among these is the student who dominates small groups. A student like this seems totally unaware that his or her undisciplined talking robs others of an opportunity to speak. One way to handle this situation is by building the role of "time-keeper" into small groups. This person keeps an eye on the second hand of a watch and indicates when a speaker's one or two minutes are up. If this tactic fails, it is time for an after-class meeting to respectfully ask the offender to give others time to share their thoughts. You might say, "Ralph, I need your assistance. I know you are excited about this topic, but there's only so much time in small groups, and I want the others to have a chance to talk also." Often the voice of reason prevails.

To summarize the key elements of our discussion thus far, and before moving on to the teaching model for small groups, here are some questions to consider:

- What do you want to accomplish with this small-group exercise?
- How big do you want the groups to be?
- How will you get students into small groups?
- What specific guidelines will you give to students?
- How much time will be allowed for the entire exercise?
- How will you summarize and pull together the small-group outcomes?

Teaching Tip: Where Are You Stuck?

Fancher Wolfe, a professor of economics, uses this simple group exercise to help him assess how well students understand assigned readings. Every other week, fifteen minutes before the end of class, students form small groups of four. Each person in the group has two minutes to tell others "where I am stuck"; that is, what the individual presently finds confusing. Perhaps it is an economic concept like *utility* or part of a lecture that did not make sense. If a student feels everything is clear, he or she can pass.

One student acts as timekeeper, giving everyone two minutes, if needed. Another student serves as recorder. Then the group takes three minutes to attempt to reach a consensus on a particular sticking point. Wolfe then asks each group's recorder to report back to the larger group. Wolfe takes notes while the others are reporting and then uses this information to address "where folks are stuck" at the next class.

Teaching Model: Using Small Groups in a Large Lecture Science Class

Two colleagues team-teach 120 students in a course entitled "Algebra-Based Physics for Nonmajors" in a traditional lecture hall. They use small groups to help students learn the basic principles of physics by observing a demonstration and trying to predict its outcome. Also, an overhead projector and a grease pencil are on hand so that the instructor can write down the students' predictions. The only preparation required is making sure that all the necessary demonstration equipment is ready. Before groups are formed, students are shown the apparatus and its various functions are explained. Then they are told how the demonstration will proceed and are asked to predict what will happen and why. For example, what happens as we pump the air out of a sealed bell jar with a ringing alarm clock inside?

Forming small groups is relatively easy. Because students attend lectures four times a week without assigned seats, group membership varies. The instructors have found that using informal groups of three works best. Starting with the first row, they ask individual students to turn around and form a group of three with the row behind them. Things are somewhat confusing the first time, but students soon get the idea.

Students receive some simple guidelines for group interaction, such as how to allow equal time for everyone's contribution and how to reach a consensus. After four to five minutes of small-group discussions, the instructors call on some representatives from the groups to share what they predicted and their rationales. These predictions are written down on the overhead transparency and the instructors ask if any groups came up with different conclusions. When all predictions are made, the class votes for a "class prediction." Then the experiment is performed. If the class prediction proves wrong, the groups must reconvene to explain what was wrong with their reasoning.

This activity has a number of advantages. When students work in small groups to make predictions, they are actively and cognitively involved in the demonstration. They have a stake in it. They are actually excited about the outcome and learn to discover gaps in their knowledge and errors in their thinking. Demonstration predictions reduce daydreaming and increase critical and creative thinking. Higher-order thinking also takes place in such a setting.

A supportive atmosphere is critical for successful prediction demonstrations. Making predictions about unfamiliar concepts in physics is risky. The cooperative nature of the small groups reduces some of the fears about taking such risks as students share ideas, make mistakes together, and have the support of the group in thinking things through. They also share their feelings of confusion, frustration, and triumph as their group prediction is tested during the experiment. A final advantage of this activity is the immediate feedback students receive as they observe the experiment and see how well their predictions turned out. More time is spent after the demonstration discussing what actually happened and why.

The major disadvantage is the time the exercise requires. Clearly, fewer topics will be covered in the lecture time. However, the topics that are covered will be better learned and remembered by the majority of students.

Final Thoughts

Informal small groups are a relatively low-risk way for teachers who are new to active learning to encourage students to assume more responsibility for their learning. Small groups work because they incorporate the key elements of active learning and lend themselves to a variety of purposes. Therefore, we should know what we want students to get out of an exercise (such as practice in summarizing, generating ideas, or comparing and contrasting points of view) and how we expect them to interact; also, we need to tell them why we are using groups. By talking and listening to one another, and by reflecting in small-group discussions, students can clarify their thinking and appreciate the perspectives of others. And once some skill in small-group participation has been mastered, students and teachers are prepared to move on to a more challenging form of active learning—cooperative student projects.

FIVE

Cooperative
Student Projects

As we suggested earlier, active learning takes place when we step out of the spotlight and help our students take more responsibility for their learning. The topic of this chapter—cooperative student projects—once again allows teachers a chance to be directors and choreographers of their students' learning. The scripting for cooperative work projects, while a bit more complex than for informal small groups, promises a full range of active-learning experiences and offers a variety of challenging roles and tasks for students.

Before proceeding to explore those roles and tasks, we need to add a few more words about terminology. We are well aware that among some active-learning advocates, the words *cooperative* and *collaborative* have different meanings—though in much of the literature that distinction is unclear. Although we appreciate the differences of opinion about terminology, we do not want to muddy the waters for readers by attempting to make fine distinctions, when it seems to us that the thrust of cooperative and collaborative learning is essentially the same. We have chosen the term *cooperative* because the work of Roger and David Johnson has influenced us in our attempts to describe what happens in cooperative groups. Thus, we will stay out of the definitional fray and stick with *cooperative learning*. The term *collaborative* will enter our discussion only when we cite others who prefer that term.

What Happens in Cooperative Student Projects

From the perspective of learning outcomes, cooperative projects and informal small groups share certain similarities: students have opportunities (1) to clarify their thinking through talking and writing, (2) to test their ideas against other students, (3) to appreciate new perspectives, and (4) to practice group-communication skills. However, cooperative projects ask students to practice, at a higher level, positive interaction and individual accountability, as well as more sophisticated group-processing skills. And as we mentioned earlier, cooperative groups work together over a longer period, such as several weeks or an entire semester, toward a shared goal. These groups might work together on a project for which students receive a common grade, or they might provide feedback that will enhance individual student projects or papers. Some features that taken as a whole distinguish cooperative student projects from informal small groups are as follows:

- Members are more dependent on the entire group for successfully completing a given task.
- Members may be assigned different tasks, based on individual skills, that contribute to group projects or tasks.
- The nature of the learning task is somewhat more complex and groups may meet outside of class, as well as in it.
- The social skills required go beyond those of listening and clarifying. They involve giving and receiving positive feedback as well as developing skills in critiquing the group process as a whole.
- Teachers serve as co-learners or master learners by helping groups stay on track and by providing resources to accomplish group tasks.

Roger Johnson and David Johnson, two internationally known researchers on cooperative learning, stress five key elements to consider in thinking about the use of cooperative groups. We will explore those elements in some depth here and then consider their practical applications in the remainder of the chapter.

1. *Positive interdependence:* Students need to know that the group cannot succeed unless each member contributes. In other words, they "sink or swim together" (Johnson, Johnson, and Smith, 1990, p. 1). Positive interdependence means that although individual students may fulfill different roles and tasks, they must depend on

each other in pursuing a common goal. Teachers need to reinforce that bond by providing clear group instructions and group rewards (Slavin, 1983, p. 439). When positive interdependence is working, students are sharing resources, providing mutual support, and celebrating their common achievement (Johnson, Johnson, and Johnson Holubec, 1990, p. 11).

2. *Individual accountability:* Students need to be responsible for their individual contributions to a group project. Thus, teachers must structure some guidelines for different components of a cooperative project, spell out specific tasks and due dates, and encourage individual accountability in regard to group efforts. Although groups will develop their own consciousness and ways of reinforcing individual accountability (and we want to encourage these student initiatives), sometimes teachers need to help by creating reasonable consequences, so that no one "hitchhikes" on the work of others. What teachers fear most about the cooperative process is that some students will not pull their own weight. The concern is a real one. To get at this issue, some teachers distribute biweekly rating sheets on which students are asked to grade themselves and each other on their individual contributions to a common project. One way to have students assess their own work is to answer questions like "What, specifically, did I contribute to this cooperative project in terms of research, writing, and organization?" or "Did I carry my fair share of the workload?" By carefully structuring group objectives and assessment tools, and by assigning well-defined individual roles and tasks, we can create an environment in which students quickly realize that their best individual efforts are necessary for the group to succeed (Slavin, 1983, p. 441). When groups fail in this regard, the teacher can always step in and serve as a mediator.

3. *Face-to-face interactions:* One great benefit of small-group interaction is the clarifying process that occurs when students explain to each other how they approached a given assignment or task. Talking things through allows students to deal with problems they may be having with a given task. It also gives the group a chance to provide valuable feedback and assistance to its troubled members. Students must allow each member of the group equal "air time" as a way of clarifying individual thinking and reinforcing a

positive environment for face-to-face interaction. Another important facet of these interactions is that they provide opportunities for
group members to support and encourage each other, as well as to
hold each other accountable. In this regard, teachers serve as role
models by the way we encourage classroom questions and support
students in clarifying their concerns.

4. *Interpersonal and small-group skills:* We cannot assume
that students have all the necessary group-interaction skills from the
outset. It helps to provide them with written guidelines such as the
Rules for Writers and Readers shown later in this chapter and to
model these social skills in our own teaching. As Harvey Weiner has
observed, "Students put into groups are only students grouped and
are not collaborators, unless a task that demands consensual learning unifies the group activity" (Weiner, 1986, p. 55). It takes some
time for students to realize that they are central to the learning
process, because they have learned to think of teachers as the true
source of wisdom. In learning to rely on each other, students often
need to figure out how to encourage the participation of their peers,
disagree without "putting down," actively listen to each other, and
ensure that everyone gets a chance to participate meaningfully.
Many teachers who use cooperative strategies specifically address
the importance of students' developing good interpersonal skills in
the course syllabus.

5. *Group processing:* Finally, groups need to assess their success and failure by learning to evaluate what they are doing well and
not so well. After students have spent a week working together in
groups, teachers can call a time-out and pose some simple group-
evaluation questions. This allows the group to reflect on their interactions thus far. Johnson, Johnson, and Johnson Holubec suggest providing time in class for groups to answer questions such as
"What individual contributions were helpful or not helpful?"
"What do we need to change in order to do a better job in the weeks
ahead?" and "Is everyone contributing their share to the group?"
(1990, p. 15). When students are given help in asking these questions, they learn how to better monitor their group's progress. Our
job, then, is to observe group interactions and to intervene when it
is clear that students cannot work things out for themselves. During

a given quarter, teachers might plan two or three time-outs for groups to assess their progress.

Teaching Tip: He Isn't Doing His Work
Students new to cooperative groups may think that it is improper or "tattling" when they complain about others not doing their share of the work. One way to get students into a positive frame of mind about responsibilities within groups is to talk about such problems before the groups get going. For example, ask students these questions: "What would you do if a group member failed to get her assignment done for next week's project?" and "What if someone doesn't contribute to small-group discussion?" List all responses on the board. Then help students see which ones are the most likely to get the best results. Asking "What can we do to help you contribute to next week's assignment?" or "What do you think about this reading assignment?" are better approaches for students, obviously, than threatening to "tell the teacher" or shaming someone who is not participating.

A significant advantage of using cooperative projects is that they can create a more congenial atmosphere for learning than traditional approaches, where students often find themselves in competition for scarce resources (such as good grades). Linda Scott and Patricia Heller warn that the competitive environment often prevailing in traditional science classes "can inhibit learning by students who may lack self-confidence in their abilities, such as female and minority students" (Scott and Heller, 1991, p. 24). In this same regard, a growing body of literature supports the use of cooperative-learning strategies for teaching culturally diverse students. Some writers suggest that Latino, American Indian, and African American students, whose cultural values and historical experiences emphasize cooperation, will find themselves more at ease learning through cooperative projects than through traditional competitive approaches (Vasquez, 1990; Little Soldier, 1989; Stikes, 1984). As

Barbara Leigh Smith and Jean T. MacGregor note, collaborative learning "invites students to build closer connections to other students, to their faculty, to their courses, and to their learning" (Smith and MacGregor, 1992, p. 11).

Many adult students also take naturally to cooperative-learning efforts because they have learned cooperative skills already in their careers. Of course, younger students will need these skills when they graduate and move into their own careers, but initially, they may need a little more direction to get started than adults (Sheridan, Byrne, and Quina, 1989, p. 51; Sharan, 1980, p. 249). As Kenneth Bruffee observes, "Collaborative learning calls on levels of ingenuity and inventiveness that many students never knew they had. And it teaches effective interdependence in an increasingly collaborative world that today requires greater flexibility and adaptability to change than ever before" (Bruffee, 1987, p. 47). While we heartily agree with that observation, to beginners, integrating cooperative learning into their normal expectations of classroom learning can seem a pretty difficult assignment. If group tasks are not clearly organized, students may leave the classroom with few good things to say about their cooperative efforts, no matter what the experts claim.

Before plunging our students into cooperative work, we need to appreciate its complexity. The initial design of work groups is a challenging enterprise. But, as we have said before, an advanced degree in group dynamics is not required to use cooperative groups. We can ease into this process by first learning to use informal small groups and then moving our students into cooperative-group tasks at the less complicated end of the scale.

The Purposes of Cooperative Student Projects

Much of the early work on cooperative learning has occurred in the context of primary and secondary education. Researchers such as the Johnsons (Johnson and others, 1981) and Robert Slavin (1980, 1983) have told the story of cooperative learning and documented its effectiveness over traditional teaching modes in improving student achievement. In addition to increasing basic thinking skills such as retention or recall, the evidence is that cooperative learning

Teaching Tip: Processing Group Success
Laurinda Porter takes some time at the first meeting
of her collaborative groups to talk about their previous group experience. She asks students to discuss
(1) previous experiences they have had with collaborative groups and their success or failure, and (2) what
new groups can do to make them run more smoothly.
By discussing their experiences and confronting potential problems directly, groups have a better chance
of avoiding common pitfalls such as absenteeism, un-
equal participation, and personality conflicts.

also promotes higher-order thinking (Johnson and others, 1981,
p. 57; Sharan, 1980, p. 251). A number of writers have indicated the
value of collaborative projects as preparation for the "real world"
(Bruffee, 1984; Sheridan, Byrne, and Quina, 1989). Also, cooperative
learning teaches important social skills and facilitates the important "social transmission" aspect of learning that Jean Piaget saw
as central to improved thinking abilities. Finally, Nancy Schniedewind and Mara Sapon-Shevin (1991) have written eloquently on the
congruity between cooperative learning and the goals of multicultural education.

It seems clear that cooperative learning can accomplish a
number of positive educational purposes. However, it is not our
purpose here to conduct a thorough review of the literature on
cooperative learning. We are convinced of its general value and
encourage readers who want a more in-depth analysis to acquaint
themselves with the resources listed in the Selected Resources for
Additional Reading and with Johnson, Johnson, and Smith's recent study, *Active Learning: Cooperation in the College Classroom*
(1991). Our intent here is to consider some of the more practical
aspects of using cooperative student projects. Cooperative learning
is a teaching tool rich with opportunity, but it also requires careful
planning on the part of teachers. If we take the time to consider our
purposes for using cooperative groups, they can create energy and

excitement in a classroom that is quite contagious. Let us be specific.

Cooperative student projects vary in complexity and in the time commitments required of students. The end results of these projects vary, too. In a history course, for example, students might be assigned to small groups and asked to analyze agricultural and population census data for different counties from 1860 to 1880. One group might focus on gathering data on the role women played in land ownership and homesteading practices; they might summarize their findings through a group presentation before the class. In another instance, students in an anthropology class might form small groups to provide feedback on the initial stages of their final research papers. Here are a few examples of other tasks such groups can accomplish:

• *Study groups:* In large classes, teachers might find it advantageous to encourage ongoing study groups that meet after class to review and summarize class readings, lectures, and the like. Guidelines can be fairly simple. A shortcoming here is that teachers cannot observe how well the groups function, but can only provide rough guidelines and try to spend some time in class helping groups consider how well they are working. In the case of adult, commuter, and working students, who may find it difficult to attend group meetings outside of scheduled class hours, teachers might need to map out some time at the end of a class period for study groups to meet.

• *Cooperative final exams:* The idea of cooperative final exams bothers many teachers who see traditional testing as one way of ensuring that individual students have done their work. On the other hand, if we consider a final exam as a means of *reinforcing learning,* what difference does it make if students take the exam cooperatively? Here, it makes sense to divide into small groups of no more than four or five, as larger groups take too long to reach consensus in their answers. On the day of the final, groups can be assigned to different parts of the classroom to work on the exam. Of course, they will need some encouragement to work quietly so they do not interfere with the work of other groups.

• *Cooperative groups to enhance individual work:* A good example here is peer writing groups. Writing groups fit naturally with most of the purposes of cooperative learning. In groups of five, students read their papers to the group and receive feedback on how well their writing communicates to others. Each student gets a chance to read and to listen and then can incorporate that feedback in papers that are submitted to the teacher for individual grading.

• *Group-graded projects:* In these projects, students work in the same small group for an entire semester and then submit their final project for a group grade. Teachers may call for smaller progressive assignments throughout the quarter that build toward the final project. In group-graded projects, explicit guidelines are crucial to the success of the project and students may be assigned different roles. Usually teachers use part of each week for the groups to meet together in class; the teachers circulate to see how the projects are progressing. Students often grade each other on individual contributions as a means of ensuring accountability.

The preceding examples suggest some specific forms cooperative work groups can take. A wide variety of projects are possible within this typology. In the next section of this chapter, we will consider concrete models of the latter two examples and show how they can be structured to ensure the best learning outcomes for students.

Structuring Cooperative Projects for Success: Teaching Models

Rather than talking on an abstract level about what teachers need to do to make sure that cooperative groups work best, this section will consider two concrete models. These models communicate the importance of having the teacher set objectives and provide guidelines for student interaction.

Peer Writing Groups for Individual Projects

Why cooperative groups work so naturally in writing classes is obvious. Most writing proceeds with a particular audience in mind, and writers want what they write to be understood by others. Thus, if they are structured appropriately, peer writing groups can go a long way toward providing opportunities for students to see and hear their own words from another person's perspective. The cooperative efforts of the group are central to this process, yet the final product—for example, a term paper—usually is graded individually.

In this type of cooperative project, positive interaction develops naturally because individuals cannot succeed without the help of others. Students quickly realize that the quality of their own writing will improve if they can hear what others are saying about it and can incorporate those comments in future drafts. To get things started, teachers usually form students into groups of four to five that stay together throughout the semester. Short papers and readings are assigned weekly, and each class begins with a mini-lecture on a specific writing problem. Then students break into small groups and read their papers aloud. They comment on each other's papers based on the teacher's focus in the mini-lecture. By participating in this process, students have the opportunity to:

- Hear how their own words sound when read by others
- Appreciate how well they succeeded in communicating to others
- Receive suggestions for improving subsequent drafts

Individual accountability is built into peer writing groups because everyone wants to receive fair and useful responses about their writing. Thus, they strive to give the same responses to others. By reading and critiquing the writing of others, students often see problems they may be blind to in their own writing. For example, as they realize that a peer is "talking down" to the reader, students learn to look for the same weakness in their writing. To help students keep on track in their groups, teachers must model the types of questions that promote good feedback. Students need to learn the benefits of asking each other questions such as "Who is your audience?" "What did you assume about your reader's knowledge of the subject matter?" and "How can you get to the main point more quickly?"

In peer writing groups, group-interaction skills are also important, but we cannot assume that students know these skills intuitively. Teachers need to provide helpful guidelines. One important rule is to make sure everyone gets equal time to read their paper and to receive both praise and constructive criticism. Following are some guidelines from Catherine Warrick, a teacher with twenty years' experience using small groups in her writing classes. Her suggestions illustrate sound principles of positive interaction and individual accountability.

Rules for Writers

1. Ask one person in the group to read your paper. Listen carefully to the sound of your own words.
2. Listen nondefensively to the responses of your classmates. Remember, they are trying to help you communicate better.
3. Do not argue. If people ask for clarification, they are not attacking you. Hear what they are asking and try to help them understand what you are trying to say.
4. Do not be paralyzed by feedback. First drafts are almost universally horrible and need a lot of work. This is your paper, and it will be better to the degree that you incorporate your classmates' feedback.

Rules for Readers

1. You have a unique opportunity to share in the growth of classmates in your group. It is an honor and a privilege. Treat it as such by speaking with thought and respect.
2. Be honest by listening and reporting accurately the effect of the words on you. Were you excited, offended, confused, convinced? Tell the writer how the words came across to you.
3. Do not argue. You do not have to agree with what the other person is trying to communicate. If you feel there is a legitimate weakness in the presentation, say so. But do not disagree for the sake of expressing your own point of view.
4. If you see technical errors (spelling, punctuation, and so on), note them in the margin of the paper and give it to the writer after the discussion. Group time is best spent focusing on elements such as organization, idea development, and emotional content.

Warrick designed these guidelines for her composition classes, but we see their applicability to cooperative projects in other

disciplines. One of our colleagues in psychology forms collaborative groups the last four weeks of the semester so that students can
discuss and comment on each other's final research papers. He reports that the quality of his student papers has improved markedly
because the students are forced to prepare drafts four weeks before
papers are due and then must read those drafts to fellow students.
So often what bogs groups down in this type of cooperative work
is the inability of individuals to give and receive criticism construc-
tively. This applies to students working in groups to write a newspaper editorial, develop a marketing plan, or complete a biology
research project. By introducing some simple guidelines for interaction, we can help students develop valuable communication skills
they will use the rest of their lives.

**Teaching Tip: Helping Groups See
What They Have Learned**
Linda Scott uses cooperative groups in many of her
classes. She takes time each week to help groups get
a grasp of their own process by giving the groups a
handout of what she calls "sentence starters." Each
student may choose any two starters he or she likes.
They go something like this: "During the past two
weeks, I learned . . . ," "I was disappointed that . . . ,"
"I have been wondering if . . . ," "I realized that
. . . ," "I was surprised . . ." Then students are asked
to share their thoughts and assess how their group
could improve its functioning. When time permits, she
randomly calls on individuals from different groups to
share with the class what they have learned.

Before we move on to group-graded projects, a word is in
order about the size of cooperative groups. The membership of informal small groups can vary from week to week because the nature
of their tasks is often just to raise questions, clarify concepts, and
generate discussion. But because the membership in cooperative
groups remains constant throughout a semester and the nature of
their tasks is more interdependent, we need to consider the impact

of absenteeism. Cooperative groups should be large enough to function given normal student absenteeism. In groups of fewer than five
students, for example, one or two missing students might incapac-
itate a project. Cooperative projects also require different tasks from
the students, sometimes necessitating a group size of six or more.
Thus we suggest a minimum of five students for any cooperative
project.

Group-Graded Projects—Examples from Different Disciplines

A slightly different use of cooperative work groups involves designing projects in which students receive a group grade for their common efforts. This type of cooperative work seems the most daunting
and problematic to teachers. It requires a degree of risk taking because awarding a common grade to a group of students flies in the
face of one of our sacred academic cows: individualism. Yet the
simple fact is that most of what students do when they leave college
will involve working together on projects, and not competing for
grades. According to Johnson, Johnson, and Smith (1991, p. 7),
"The use of collaborative learning groups approximates more
closely the activity of real-world employment and problem-solving
[and] allows students to tackle more complicated, and often more
interesting problems without feeling overwhelmed." Playing the
rugged individualist in every classroom situation does not do much
for students when they join the work force. They need practice and
experience working in groups toward common goals.

     A few concrete examples illustrate the applicability of group-
graded projects. Sharon Bailey-Bok teaches a course in marketing
principles in which she assigns groups of students to invent a product and then create a marketing plan and present it to the class, as
they might to a company board of directors. The project is due at
the end of the semester, and it counts for one-third of a student's
final grade; the remainder results from individual tests and
problem-solving scores. Bailey-Bok provides a detailed handout
that structures the assignment and suggests different roles individuals can play in terms of research, writing, and planning strategies.
The project has two components. First, each group of five to six

students prepares a "team paper," which counts for 40 percent of their project grade. Second, the groups make presentations to the class that account for the remaining 60 percent, half of which is based on peer evaluation. The project is assigned early in the semester and provides additional motivation for students to attend class and do their assigned readings, since both are essential to a successful project.

Roseanna Ross asks students in her course, "Interpersonal Communications for Business and the Professions," to work cooperatively in teaching a few concepts to their classmates. About three weeks after the quarter starts, the class brainstorms issues (mentioned briefly in discussion or in the textbook) that students would like to pursue in depth, for example, mentoring, networking, and team building. The class votes on all the topics identified, and the top five are selected. Each student chooses one of the five topics to research (as long as five to seven students will be available as a group for each of the topics), and each group has three to four weeks to research and prepare a presentation on the topic for the class. Ross assists by suggesting resources and by providing guidelines for group interaction.

The groups meet outside of class for most of their work, though some in-class time is allowed so that Ross can circulate and see how group projects are progressing. The last two class sessions are reserved for the presentations. Each group has forty-five minutes to teach their concept to the class and to share a resource bibliography they have developed during their research. Then the class has fifteen minutes for questions and feedback. The class also completes a rating-response form. In Ross's exercise, the groups practice the communication skills learned in the course, assume responsibility for teaching others, and address some subject areas that the instructor had not originally intended to cover in such depth.

All cooperative work projects need not be so time intensive as those we have described; they also do not have to count so heavily toward a student's final grade. In Chet Meyers's natural science course, "Minnesota Fishes," students pair up to explore a local fishing lake and write a "personality profile" of that lake's limnological, biological, and fishing characteristics. Each team of students submits one four- to five-page paper, for which they receive a common grade that counts 20 percent toward their final evaluation.

We might mention here that while it takes time to begin trusting students and to develop meaningful cooperative projects, students really seem to enjoy these endeavors. In a more collegial atmosphere students are often freer to experiment, try new ideas, and express different points of view. Another advantage of cooperative projects is the efficiency they provide teachers vis-à-vis grading. Dividing a class of thirty students into five teams of six greatly reduces the number of final papers or projects to be graded.

Final Thoughts

Both authors of this book are relatively new to cooperative student projects, but we can attest to their problematical nature as well as their considerable benefits. We are impressed by the enthusiasm of our more experienced colleagues and recognize the care and consideration with which they have developed cooperative projects that work. Cooperative strategies are clearly a significant aspect of the world students will enter outside of the classroom. Students need to learn how to work together and to be accountable for individual work that contributes to a common goal, for that is likely to be how they will be judged in their occupations and careers. Cooperative projects lessen the competitive atmosphere that often lies not far beneath the surface in most classes—especially with regard to tests and papers. In a cooperative atmosphere, students from diverse ethnic backgrounds, where cooperation is a shared cultural value, often feel more at home and less threatened. For all these reasons, we encourage teachers to consider ways they can begin exploring cooperative student projects.

SIX

Simulations

Simulation is an umbrella term that covers some interesting active-learning strategies—including role playing, simulation exercises and games, and computer models—that allow students to practice and apply their learning. Simulations place students in an artificially constructed, yet sufficiently realistic context for learning, a "dynamic metaphor of some slice of reality" (Palmer and Snyder, 1986, p. 16). In this context, students practice and experience, almost like apprentices in some cases, what they normally get second-hand from reading and lectures. They bridge the familiar gap between theory and practice, thus developing their own critical abilities rather than relying solely on textbook explanations and what the experts preach. Simulations give students a chance to practice the basics of active learning as they read prepared materials, talk and listen in various character roles, reflect on participation in debriefing sessions, and write up summaries of learning outcomes. When simulation strategies are used judiciously and effectively, students and teachers enthusiastically join in learning. In fact, simulations may rekindle the enthusiasm for learning that some students have lost along the way and provide a welcome relief from much of higher education's prosaic everyday pursuits.

What Are Simulations?

Because *simulation* is such a generic term, we believe it is helpful to offer brief descriptions of some types of simulations.

Role Playing

Role playing usually involves a small number of students, say two or three, or just a student and a teacher. It puts students into someone else's shoes by giving them a character to play, a scene to act, or a situation to imagine. For example, two students might act the roles of a sister and brother in a disruptive family situation. Or students can "retain their own roles and behavior patterns, but act as if they were in a different situation" (Shannon, 1986, pp. 27–34). In this instance, pairs of students in a communication-skills course might advise each other about which classes to take the next term as a means of assessing how well each listens and offers advice. Role plays like this give students a chance to try out theories and techniques that have been covered formally in reading assignments or lectures.

Simulation Exercises and Simulation Games

These terms generally refer to situations in which a whole class is involved, with students assuming different roles as they act out a prescribed scenario. These scenarios incorporate specific rules and activities designed to teach a concept or to have students put a theory into practice. As examples, students in a course on state and local government might participate in a simulated school-board meeting concerned with raising taxes to pay for educational programs; human service administration students might simulate a planning session in a community mental health program; environmental science students might act as an advisory team brought in as consultants during a major oil spill; and business students might take sides in a stockholders' meeting concerned with a leveraged buyout. In simulation exercises like these, students must operate within the limits of the knowledge they have obtained from reading assignments and lectures and must abide by any ground rules for interaction spelled out by their teacher. In some exercises and games, students might be "put into a position of physically feeling an abstract concept, such as discrimination" (Shannon, 1986, p. 27). Simulation games often are similar in basic format to board games and game packages with which we are all familiar, such as Monopoly or Risk. Simulation games tend to have "winners" and "losers," so that competition is a factor in the classroom and sometimes must be controlled if it gets in the way of learning. A number of simulation games can be purchased or teachers can try a hand at designing their own (Hyman, 1981; Jones, 1985, 1988; Greenblatt, 1987).

Computer Models

Computer models are—you guessed it—simulation exercises and games designed as software packages for computers. As we will note in this chapter and in Chapter Nine, the use of computers in the active-learning classroom has its share of pluses and minuses (Schick, 1990). For the moment, however, looking at the advantages, computer simulations create environments, situations, and games that incorporate more detail and data than printed versions. Like simulation exercises and games, computer versions allow students to deal with some practical, problem-solving experiences, as well as to practice skills "that are either too dangerous, too expensive, or too remote and inaccessible for humans to encounter directly" (Bok, 1985, p. 6).

The sciences, such as chemistry, are a good example of how a well-designed computer simulation can allow students to work with potentially hazardous chemicals without explosive consequences, how biologists can set up work with distant animal populations and environments that are inaccessible to students attending a city college, or how students in physics can initiate and interact with demonstrations without the need for a costly research facility. Depending on space and equipment, students can work in pairs, in small groups, or through computer networks to encourage discussion and interaction. The liquid-crystal display (LCD) makes it possible to project what appears on a computer screen to a larger group, thus giving the entire class a chance to watch and participate in the activities. Also, computers can be used effectively as elements of a simulation game or exercise as the following teaching tip illustrates.

Despite enthusiastic reports and supporters, using computer models for simulation requires some caution. Availability and cost of computers aside, it takes a large investment of time to construct a viable computer program for simulation—perhaps up to two hundred hours of preparations. Not everyone will have access to the necessary equipment and space designed for students working to-

Teaching Tip: Computer Data Assist
Professor Gabriel G. Manrique's international-trade students only have access to a few personal computers in their classroom. He prepares a spreadsheet that incorporates economic and trade data on six nations or groups of nations that students will represent in simulated trade negotiations. The spreadsheet is designed to operate with just a few keystrokes on the part of the students, because the focus of the simulation is on the negotiating process, not the computer. Toward the middle of the term, students receive a computer disk containing the spreadsheet for the nations they represent. At the end of the term, the simulated negotiations occur. The computer spreadsheet is used only to facilitate calculations of offers and counteroffers. The face-to-face negotiations are the focus of this simulation. By virtue of the spreadsheets, students can concentrate on looking at effects and formulating responses rather than spending an inordinate amount of time on calculations.

gether with computers, even if the costs are reasonable. In addition, the facility with which computer simulations can replicate actual hands-on experience with tools of the trade can be a mixed blessing. In the sciences, for example, Prudy Hall suggests an important question: Will computer simulations rob students of the opportunity to develop certain mechanical skills and firsthand working experience with live organisms? Indeed, if the lab experiences of students in the sciences are deferred too long by computer simulation, how will students discover whether they dislike the laboratory aspects so central to careers in the sciences?

Still, all in all, computer simulations offer a creative and expanding resource for learning that is valuable, especially for teachers and students in small schools with limited physical resources in the sciences and other disciplines. Each issue of *The Chronicle of Higher Education* generally carries handy summaries of software for new computer simulations and more extended descriptions of simulation projects under the headings "Computer Software" and "Information Technology."

Now that we have described some of the varied types of simulation, let us move on to consider what students will experience and learn.

What Happens in Simulations?

Role playing and simulation exercises and games aim at "a representation of a real world event in a reduced and compressed form that is dynamic, safe, and efficient" (Rockler, 1978, p. 288). Also, simulations transport our students into roles and situations that involve relatively low risks for those who are shy and reluctant to participate. Stephen D. Brookfield points out that in contrast to reading or listening, good simulations will "involve the whole person—intellect, feeling, and bodily senses" so that what students learn will "be experienced more deeply and remembered longer" (Brookfield, 1990, p. 115). And the more realistic a simulation is, the more students will appreciate the importance and relevance of their learning. In a simulation, students might confront discrimination, make political decisions, model a different style of communication, counsel a chronically depressed patient, and, perhaps with the aid of a computer model, plan military strategy for Civil War campaigns. With such a range of possibilities, simulations are bound to increase student motivation, as well as heighten cooperation and interaction among students (Dorn, 1989, pp. 6–8).

What do students learn and gain from simulations? Because simulations require the personal involvement of participants, students are forced to think on their feet, question their own values and responses to situations, and consider new ways of thinking. Thus, they learn in ways that traditional teaching approaches seldom can accomplish. For example, one of our colleagues uses role playing in his "Counseling Theories" course. He asks one student to assume the role of counselor and to apply Carl Rogers' methodology in working with another student "client," who is experiencing mid-life crisis. The class observes the role play and then critiques it. By having the students do this, the teacher forces the class to grapple with and apply theories of counseling on a different level than they would reach by writing an essay test or analytical paper.

Another important outcome for students, particularly in role-playing situations, is the development of empathy. In a collective-bargaining simulation (one of the first widely used simulation exercises), students often get wrapped up in the negotiations and find themselves enmeshed in the problems and emotions experienced by either the management or labor teams. Sara Rasch, a colleague in management, not only uses a standard collective-bargaining simulation in her course, but, after students have completed the simulation, she has them reverse roles so they can understand what it is like to be on the opposite side of the negotiating table. By playing *both* roles, students learn to have empathy for two very different perspectives and see that there are seldom either-or answers to problems in the workaday world.

By combining role play with in-class writing assignments, teachers can use simulations to encourage similar reflection. In her European history class, Professor Loretta T. Johnson has devised what might be seen as an ongoing role play for students. After some introductory remarks and reading about eighteenth-century European thought and society, tied to the outbreak of the French Revolution, she asks students to create their own character—any gender, religion, class, or means of livelihood—who was born in France between 1770 and 1780. Students write out a description in class of their character's personality and role in society. In succeeding classes, Johnson periodically asks the students to describe their character's actions or reactions to the events and circumstances of the French Revolution. As the students write more about their characters, the readings and information in the course acquire more immediacy and interest. Johnson's students are consciously and continually analyzing the effect of a historical event on specific individuals and the impact of those individuals on events.

Perhaps the best way to illustrate the variety of learning outcomes simulations yield is through a multidimensional example. In her course, "The Nurse as Communicator," Mary Overvold-Ronnigen has created a midterm simulation in which students assume the role of nurses during an intake interview. After studying three classic types of patients that nurses often encounter and are expected to recognize, Overvold-Ronnigen's students know they could be meeting a client who suffers from depression, withdrawal, or anxiety. Specially trained students from another class can play the role of the patients (Lane, 1988). The entire simulation lasts fifteen minutes and is videotaped.

The student nurse enters the intake room and meets the patient. Through a series of her own questions and through observation, the student must decide which behavior pattern the patient exhibits. She then writes up her observations to present to her "supervisor" (the instructor). In this simulation, the nursing student practices key elements of that profession: proper intake procedures, communication and interviewing skills, intervention skills, empathic communication, preliminary diagnostic skills, and writing of case notes. On a more general scale, the simulation involves students in listening, analyzing, using clear written and verbal communication, reflecting, and solving problems.

For the final part of the simulation, the student and instructor observe the videotape and students have the opportunity to reassess their original conclusions and critique their performance—*before* the instructor does the same. Students might, for example, see on the tape errors they made during the initial intake procedure. That is fine, so long as the students catch them.

While the foregoing is an example of a detailed, time-intensive simulation, it encapsulates the wealth of learning possibilities simulations offer. It also demonstrates why some instructors feel so strongly about including simulations as part of their teaching repertoires.

In summary, simulations challenge students' current ways of thinking and allow them to:

- Practice a *general skill* (such as interviewing or nonverbal communication)
- Practice a *specific skill* (such as Rogerian counseling)
- Practice *team skills* (such as collective bargaining)
- Develop *problem-solving skills* (such as a computerized simulation of a physics experiment)
- Engage in *synthesizing skills* (such as dealing with a management problem described in a text, but not discussed in class)

- Develop *basic empathic skills* (such as imagining the woes of a peasant in the French Revolution)
- Develop *advanced empathic skills* by turning around and assuming the opposite side (such as students in a collective bargaining simulation reversing roles)

Because simulations are often so thought-provoking and intensive, students can get carried away. Teachers need to set up clear guidelines and ground rules *specific to each type of simulation* so that things do not get out of control.

Structuring Simulations for Success

Many aspects of small-group learning are present in simulations, though the dynamics may be heightened a bit. It requires a lot of "letting go" by teachers for students to learn effectively from a simulation or a role play. The risks are high for teachers, and it is natural to feel a bit squeamish as we watch students struggle to assume their various roles. So if we feel uneasy letting students work in small groups for ten minutes, turning them loose for an entire sixty-minute class in a simulated collective-bargaining session or a constitutional convention could truly test our nerves.

We offer these comments not as a discouragement, but as an honest acknowledgment that using simulations requires a good deal of personal confidence on our part as teachers. But again, as with small-group exercises, the opportunity for higher levels of learning and broader participation among students makes the risk of conducting simulations well worth it. And by our recognizing some of the pitfalls associated with simulations, the possibility of successful outcomes may be increased.

Here are a few considerations to keep in mind so that we can ensure a positive learning experience. First of all, it is always important to set aside adequate class time, both for the actual activity and for discussion and debriefing. Nothing is more frustrating for students than to get wrapped up in a simulation and not have enough time to complete it and talk about what happened during it. Without our leadership to help students extract learning from a game or role play, the activity becomes just a token gesture at active learning—a fun event, but not educationally sound. In the case of computer simulations, unless students have been working in teams or pairs, the postsimulation discussion and debriefing may be the only time they have a chance to consolidate what they have experienced.

Debriefing time allows students to reflect on their participation in the simulation and on how well they achieved the simulation's objectives. Teachers can pose questions such as, How did the simulation give you opportunities to apply what we have been discussing in class? What worked especially well in the simulation? or What went wrong? For students new to simulations, debriefing is doubly important because it gives teachers time to reiterate what they hoped to achieve and it provides helpful feedback to students so that they can participate successfully in future simulations.

Another element of successful simulations is knowing how to encourage students who tend to be passive, easily frustrated, and reluctant to join in. The classroom atmosphere must be supportive for students so that they will "feel free to assess themselves, to try out new behaviors and attitudes, and to provide and receive feedback from each other on the results of their experience" (Bowen, 1987, p. 197). A good technique to help create this supportive atmosphere is for teachers to participate in the role playing or games. James B. M. Schick makes the suggestion that when teachers "play their role to the hilt," perhaps by wearing a costume in a simulation or by adopting an accent, some of the passive, quiet students will be emboldened and "lose their reluctance to involve themselves" (Schick, 1990, p. 117). We have observed this phenomenon in our own classroom activities. Teacher participation also alleviates stage fright by helping students to see that making mistakes is part of the exercise and not a cause for embarrassment.

Here are some additional tips for encouraging participation. Starting out slowly with a few simple role plays for our braver students and working up to exercises involving all members of the class makes sense (Shannon, 1986, p. 101). Freezing the action during a role play or exercise, so that class members can make suggestions and helpful comments, will take some of the pressure off students directly involved in any activity (Bowen, 1987; Nyquist and Wulff, 1990, p. 353). Finally, suspending grades for students' performance in a simulation encourages participation because it reduces the pressure of performing well.

The teacher's role in simulations requires considerable preparation and follow-up. However, some guidelines from those who use simulations frequently can save us a lot of grief. Here are some points the experts advise us to keep in mind:

- Observe before you use simulations. If at all possible, sit in on a colleague's class where simulations are used routinely and observe how a simulation works and how students behave.
- Know how a simulation fits within the overall goals for a course. Tread softly at first and resist the temptation to overuse simulation strategies at the expense of teaching approaches that are more appropriate to certain situations and topics. For example, a number of simulations scheduled in the first few weeks of an advanced class in the sciences would likely fall flat if students needed time to review basic concepts and methodology.
- Prepare well in advance. Brief students about expectations, rules, and so on and know the game or role-playing situation inside out. You might run through the exercise with a colleague before trying it out on a class so that the snags are evident.
- Plan class periods with plenty of time to spare for discussion and debriefing.
- Match up simulations with the students' abilities, preparation, and maturity in a discipline. Do not put them in over their heads. In role plays, do not overload or shortchange students with detail.
- Make sure that preassignments and follow-up assignments enhance and extend what students do in the simulations (Dorn, 1989; Shannon, 1986; Hyman, 1981).
- Play the role of moderator or rules adviser when necessary, but do not intrude on the process if things are going smoothly.
- Terminate the simulation action at a high point so that discussion will be charged with a high interest level and excitement (Klemer and Smith, 1975).
- Remember that the postsimulation discussion and analysis is every bit as important as the activity itself. Help students see

what a role play or simulation game can suggest for subsequent learning.

- Set up discussion and postsimulation analysis so that you can have a firsthand idea about the pros and cons of the activity from your students. Try to debrief yourself right after the class period. Take notes about what works and what falls flat.

Teaching Models: Community Development and Student Writing

Here are two teaching models that serve as examples of a simulation game and a role-playing exercise. Both models, though they differ in subject matter, illustrate how simulations work and provide some general principles and ideas that can be put to use in a classroom.

The Machakos Simulation Game

Tom O'Toole teaches a course on the political economy of Africa. To give his students practical experience as volunteers in rural development, he uses the Machakos Village Development Game his department has purchased. This simulation game allows students to take part in four phases of the community development process within some villages of Central Kenya. Student teams assist Kenyan villagers in development, and the simulation concludes with shared reflections about the experience.

In phase one of the game, students get an idea of what the village development volunteer's life is like through a simulated environment (the room is carefully prepared and features photos, artwork, fabric hangings, articles of clothing, drums, baskets, and music), orientation slides, and scripted situations. The students experience a shift of cultural context and get a feel for the hopes and dreams of the villagers. They also get a glimpse of the obstacles they will confront in their roles as volunteers.

In subsequent phases of the simulation game, students are introduced to the mechanics of the game, participate in team meetings and other exercises, and build a strategy for completing multiple grass-roots–generated projects to strengthen the capacity for

self-sufficiency in villages. They also view slides of village subloca-
tions and reflect on their experience of working in rural Kenya.
This process of reflection proceeds in relation to personal values,
societal institutions, home communities, views about the world,
cooperative work toward a common goal, and the interrelations of
peoples around the world.

Throughout the experience, students feel the frustrations and
exhilarations of the volunteer's work. Through reflective conversations and debriefing, they see how complex the development process
is, how teamwork plays an important part, and how long-range
benefits result from the villagers' participation in activities. To encourage participation without pressure, the teamwork and interaction of students is not evaluated for grading; however, graded
papers are assigned asking students to analyze and summarize their
reactions to the simulation game. Also, students create their own
fact-and-fiction scenario that is graded and applies what they have
learned about aspects of development in the Machakos area.

O'Toole finds that the greatest strength of the simulation
game is that it feels so real to students. Students have little difficulty
imagining themselves being there. The game shares with all good
simulations the chance to experience, not just learn about, a piece
of real life. It differs from most because it includes an unusual
amount of detail about a real place and an actual process. As
O'Toole notes, the game is time-consuming and complex, but the
reactions of his students are very positive. As one said: "I learned
more during the four-hour period by playing the game than I did
in many of the prior lectures." In the simulation, this student discovered obstacles and problems in the development process that she
would normally never have imagined.

Role Play and Writing

All freshman English students at Deana Evans's university share a
common reading experience in their first quarter of study. The
"common reader" is Leslie Stevenson's *Seven Theories of Human
Nature* (1987). In this book, seven theories about human nature that
have shaped Western thought are represented, including Marxism.

Students are expected to write a five-hundred-word paper based on their reading and in-class discussions. Evans uses a simple role play to help clarify a chapter dealing with Marxism in the assigned reading and suggests alternative views.

To begin the role play, each student in Evans's class selects a partner. Then each pair receives a task sheet with these instructions: "Imagine that you are the individual described below and that Karl Marx, either in person or in a dream, appears to advise you. Write one paragraph summarizing the advice you think Marx would offer." Each task sheet describes a fictitious person who will meet up with Marx, including some who might be attracted to his ideas and some who would not. Each pair must discuss the hypothetical conversation and jointly construct a paragraph that summarizes what Marx's advice might be. While students are discussing and writing their paragraphs, Evans circulates around the room, answering questions and offering suggestions.

At the next class session, one student in each pair reads the description of the fictitious person; the other reads the advice that Marx might give. The rest of the students in the class ask questions and discuss the issues that arise. When each student finally tackles the five-hundred-word essay, the simulation and class discussions form a basis for writing by providing ideas and examples about what many find a difficult topic, obscured by stereotypes of Marxism. As a result, Evans finds that her students can write a better essay on the appeal of Marxism for individuals in a variety of historical situations; also, they use more examples in their papers in support of generalizations.

While composition theorists agree, in general, that student writers need to be more involved in their writing tasks, teachers seldom consider role-playing assignments as options. The oversight is unfortunate, because by definition, role plays require intimate involvement with the subject and active participation. They also stimulate imaginative and critical thinking. Reading assignments that some students view with hostility at first become interesting and often exciting material for class discussions and writing tasks. Students also get immediate feedback on their initial ideas and approaches to writing the assignment.

Final Thoughts

Most experts warn that simulations can be overused in the classroom. Simulations, in general, should be brought in sparingly and not become an end in themselves. The danger here is that students can get caught up solely in the novelty and fun of an activity and, in the process, fail to see the learning goals we are trying to achieve.

Some types of simulation are easier for teachers and students to handle than others. A simple role play observed by the class is easier to pull off than a full-scale simulation game for the entire class. Some disciplines match up more easily with simulations than others—communications, psychology, management, and sociology come to mind. But with some creativity, teachers of most academic stripes can create their own interesting and useful simulations.

In addition, we need to acknowledge that simulations are not value-free and might undercut some of the goals we hope active learning will achieve (Dorn, 1989, p. 8). For example, if we are not careful, simulation games might go too far and encourage too much competition among students. In such instances, winning can take precedence over learning and the students may miss an academic point entirely.

Finally, take comfort in the fact that giving simulations a try, even if you only use one role play during a semester, can lead to a more interactive classroom. Talk to colleagues who have used simulations in their classes. Do your preparation. But take the leap. You may be pleasantly surprised with the outcome, and your students may just find the experience one of the most memorable and educational they have encountered in a long time.

SEVEN

Case Studies

Case studies and active learning fit together hand and glove. A successful case study involves many features characteristic of active learning: student-teacher interaction, collaboration, problem solving, reflection, and extensive discussion. Within a case study framework, students develop group-interaction skills, respond to ideas and contributions of classmates, and apply career and life experiences. Another value of a case study is its potential for involving students in discussions that call for higher-order levels of reasoning, such as analyzing situations, forming judgments, and evaluating solutions. For teachers, the case study method is a stimulating training ground for *guiding* student learning and interaction, as opposed to *enforcing* it.

We usually identify case studies with the method pioneered at the Harvard Business School, and justifiably so, although the idea has proved easily adaptable to many academic disciplines (Christensen and Hansen, 1987). In its most recognizable form, a case study is a narrative of an actual event that brings students and teachers together in an attempt to examine, discuss, and advance solutions to a realistic problem situation. A case study usually involves written materials that require analysis and "provide fodder for a rich discussion" (Hansen, 1987, p. 264).

A case study is designed so that students can identify with a situation and the actors described in it. In other words, students can envision themselves as part of a case study because it offers a "dimension of realism so often lacking in the structured learning milieu" (Fisher, 1978, p. 259). At a basic level, a case study sets up a problem to be solved or a question to be answered. The best of case studies present a "dilemma, a knotty problem" that teachers hope

will "provoke radically different responses and suggestions for action from students" (Myers and Weeks, 1974, p. 1). Finally, case
studies usually are open-ended. Students engaged in a case study
must reach decisions about how to solve a particular problem,
realizing that no one solution is correct. In certain disciplines, such
as the sciences and other technical subjects, although correct solutions must be revealed, case study discussion still can be presented
as open-ended in the discussion phase.

As a teaching strategy, case studies have attracted considerable attention from educational writers and researchers; indeed, the
literature is overflowing with publications and exemplary models.
To consolidate this information, let us start with a concrete example from our own teaching experience. A simple case study narrative
of an actual classroom experience should make the bulk of information and description in this chapter easier to follow and digest.

> "Leota Shaw," a working adult student in her late
> fifties, presented quite a difficult teaching problem in
> Thomas Jones's diplomatic history class. Shaw had
> enrolled in the class purely for enjoyment and because
> she had read quite a bit on her own about contempo-
> rary foreign-policy issues. Right from the start, she
> joined enthusiastically in classroom discussions and
> small-group exercises. However, her participation in
> the first two simulated historical situations seemed to
> bother her classmates and caused her professor con-
> cern as well. Shaw routinely ignored the role specif-
> ically detailed by the assignment. For example, ten
> minutes into the first simulation, instead of playing
> the part of a foreign-policy adviser in the Kennedy
> administration, she said, "Professor Jones, I know
> from page 44 of today's reading assignment that
> Kennedy depended heavily for advice on this issue
> from his brother, the attorney general." To make her
> point crystal-clear, Shaw then started reading out loud
> from the text. Jones reminded her gently that she
> needed to stay in character for the simulation. Five
> minutes later, she broke in with a direct quote drawn

from her other readings, again deflating the mood and intent of the exercise. A couple of weeks later, and despite renewed instructions to students about how to participate in a simulation exercise, Shaw delivered a set of opinions to the class as they attempted another simulation exercise. Although her comments made sense as historical analysis, she had interrupted the simulation again. On this occasion, Jones noticed considerable eye-rolling and visible hostility from other members of the class. Jones had hoped to use this kind of simulation throughout the course, but Shaw's actions posed an impediment to his teaching plans and to the learning environment he was trying to create.

At this point, readers are probably asking what Jones did to solve this teaching dilemma. Some may be thinking about what they might do, or what they did when they experienced a similar situation. Others may be considering what additional information is necessary to better understand the circumstances and principles involved in this classroom episode. These are exactly the kinds of questions and reactions that a case study tries to set off among participants. If, as fellow teachers, we had the chance to gather in a seminar to consider this case, we would likely proceed to enthusiastically examine, discuss, and advance solutions to this realistic teaching problem. It invites our interest and our attempts at resolution.

Perhaps this brief example will suggest to you some possibilities for using case studies in courses you teach. As an active-learning strategy, the case study approach is congenial to a variety of academic disciplines. At our university, several courses use case studies: for example, journalism students consider how a woman editor can deal with sexist language practiced by reporters on the sports page, a class in gerontological nursing tries to figure out how to quiet the battles and fears of two elderly sisters in the same wing of a nursing home, majors in the management program ponder the ethics of "business favors" when dealing with accounts in a foreign nation, and students in an introductory science course follow a historical narrative of the steps preceding a breakthrough discovery in medicine, then attempt to draw conclusions about what actually happened. Some of these courses incorporate role playing to enhance written case materials, enliven discussion, and put students in touch with what the main characters in a case study are experiencing.

As the foregoing suggests, case studies can be used for teaching a diversity of subjects. Teachers in different disciplines have modified the original Harvard case method, contributing refinements to the original approach. At the same time, certain fundamentals about purpose, preparation, teaching, and evaluation continue to inform the teaching of case studies. Let us consider these fundamentals and, while we are at it, explore some of the more ingenious modifications of the case method.

What Happens in a Case Study

Students follow a well-defined path in a typical case study: (1) they *receive information* about a case and study it by themselves, (2) they *participate in a group discussion,* sometimes preceded by trying out ideas in study groups, and (3) they *reflect* on the case, the discussion, and the solutions, and on their actions, attitudes, and behaviors. As an example, in a marketing seminar, students might receive case materials that tell the story of a sales representative concerned about overinflated advertising claims for a product. The seminar session would begin with students reading a series of memos about the advertising claims between the sales representative and the advertising department. The open-ended "knotty dilemma" of the case might revolve around a troubling ethical-legal decision faced by the sales representative. After some small-group discussions, the students would use the remainder of a seminar session to analyze the dilemma and discuss solutions; the instructor would serve as the discussion leader. At the end of the class, students and teacher would spend time summarizing points of view and possible solutions, as well as reflecting on how they approached the case study as individuals and as a larger group. Students could be asked to write up their observations on specific elements that surfaced in the case study discussion for the next class meeting.

Teaching by the case method is a varied and complex endeavor. For the most part, discussion leaders must stay on the sidelines when it comes to supplying answers and opinions, allowing students to take the field by themselves. At the same time, teachers define the boundaries by providing the case study materials, and they promote—and sometimes referee—the action during the all-important discussion segment. Also, teachers must create a classroom atmosphere that is "informal" and "detached" so that students share their "wisdom in a manner conducive to sound, objective decision making" (Fisher, 1978, p. 259).

While case studies routinely rely on written materials, some teachers have discovered that a dramatization, an oral report, a media presentation, or an interactive computer program can deliver all or part of the initial material needed to get discussion started. This might mean bending tradition somewhat by creating fictitious, yet realistic accounts and plausible situations. Since the ultimate goal is to have students actively involved in learning and problem solving, using a case based on hypothetical materials or even a classic of world literature makes sense. Ultimately, such variations from the norm will succeed in terms of how well they allow students to identify with situations and characters, pursue discussions, and generate solutions. Case study experts John Boehrer and Marty Linsky conclude: "A great variety of materials, real and imaginative, can serve as vehicles for enabling students to project themselves into a concrete, practical situation and to engage in productive discussion of the issues" (Boehrer and Linsky, 1990, p. 46).

Before jumping on the case study bandwagon, we need to keep in mind that in some subjects, beginning students simply will not have the knowledge base necessary to do case studies. For example, first-time students in counseling probably will not be ready for a case study on child abuse, and students in an introductory botany course will not be prepared as yet for a case study involving complex issues in genetic engineering. These students need some basic terms, concepts, theoretical background, and techniques. A successful case study experience grows out of a solid, fundamental understanding of a subject. Otherwise, the case study will fall flat and is likely to degenerate into a dispiriting bull session. Once students are prepared to participate in a case study, they should begin with simple scenarios that do not outrun their abilities. Then, as Wilbert J. McKeachie wisely suggests, cases should be sequenced in terms of their difficulty, detail, and complexity (McKeachie, 1986, p. 173). Creating a successful case study means thinking about how the material will match the level of our students' knowledge and the type of subject we teach. But when we take the time to do it right, a well-constructed case study promotes the best kind of active learning and delivers ample rewards to students and teachers alike.

Teaching Tip: Innovative Sources for Case Studies
Finding appropriate and exciting case study material outside the printed word is not as hard as it first might appear. Television news specials, public television documentaries, movies, and plays deal with a variety of issues—economic, political, moral, and psychological—that can be the basis for a case study or a stimulating companion to written materials. Earl Bolick of Metropolitan State University suggests another source of case study material close at hand: our students. In particular, adult students bring a variety of experiences from their careers, cultural backgrounds, volunteer work, community organizing, and personal experiences that can be turned into exciting materials for discussion.

The Purpose of Case Studies

The dimensions of a good case study throw a net over even the most reluctant students, eventually pulling them into discussion and problem solving with their classmates. Once a case study begins, students realize that they are the driving force, and that they must collaborate and supply the energy to make it a success. The teacher selects the case, guides the activities, and occasionally jumps in with a well-timed addition to the conversation, but the students need to make things happen in the classroom by sharing ideas and learning from each other.

In such fields as business, counseling, and education, the contributions of the case method in developing career-related skills are apparent. A good case study is often an apprenticeship of sorts. For example, students participating in a case drawn up by the Harvard Business School will be learning and applying theories and techniques they will use in the real world of business. At a safe distance, where no one will lose even a dime of the chief financial officer's budget, students get an idea of what life is like at the Acme Widgets Corporation and experience what it takes to unravel facts and figures, manage personalities, reach decisions, apply ethics, take risks, and solve problems.

In dealing with the realistic worlds brought to the classroom through case studies, students get to practice the theories and techniques that they have encountered in readings and class lectures. So, for example, the theories and techniques introduced in a lecture or small-group session can serve as the basis for a case study on nursing practices for pain management. Or a reading on sexism in education can be applied to a case study on high school teaching. The end result of this in-class practice is the development of experience that can be used outside the classroom in specific career situations.

Another advantage of the case method is that because students must work closely with specific information (such as terms, concepts, and theories), they are more likely to retain it. Retention is further enhanced because a good case study integrates concepts and techniques in a more realistic and lively fashion than textbooks and lectures do. Practically speaking, in a class on statistics, under which circumstances would students be more likely to retain information: listening to a lecture on statistical probability or joining in a case study of a blackjack player in Las Vegas attempting to beat the odds and gain a fortune? We will place our bets on the case study.

Before the teaching and learning start, a case study has to be selected and readied for the classroom well in advance. The number of published case studies is limited in most subjects except the professional fields, such as management or law. Those of us who design a case study in the humanities or social sciences may have to write most of the materials ourselves and put the instructions together. But depending on the complexity we seek, writing a case study is not as hard as it appears initially.

The case study we select or prepare should mesh with our overall teaching objectives and students' capabilities. The impression that a case study would be perfect for our class may prove correct. However, before we act on that impression, the materials need to be checked carefully. Case studies adapted from published collections must be thoroughly previewed to make sure that they address specific teaching objectives for our class. Reading a few published cases will also help us to construct our own, whether it is a full-blown case or a short scenario.

Selecting or writing a good case study also hinges on several techniques and rules. Here are some important ones to consider:

• *Cases tell a story:* They report the facts of a situation just as a news reporter would; cases flow from the premise that students need to be filled in on what is happening. Therefore, in writing cases, a teacher should not allow bias and opinionated prose to sneak into the narrative, thus leading students to some predetermined resolution the teacher has in mind (Myers and Weeks, 1974, p. 4). As Sergeant Joe Friday used to say on TV's *Dragnet:* "All I want is the facts . . . just give me the facts."

• *Cases put students into the shoes of the main characters:* They seize students' attention right away with a situation that is realistic and compelling, as the "Leota Shaw" episode may have done for our readers. A bland and contrived focus for a case study will produce like results. The ideas is to have students "stop talking about 'the case' and become immersed in the situation" (*The Case Method,* 1969, p. 3).

• *Cases should not bury students under an avalanche of information and details:* Length must be tailored to the time available, and the complexity of cases must be matched to the level of learning students have attained. Cases for beginning students should make the most important facts and issues obvious. As students grow in their sophistication in terms of what they know and how they handle case study exercises, they can advance to materials that are more complex.

Case study experts have accumulated a considerable store of information and advice about effective writing techniques. Again, the Harvard Business School leads the way with several excellent guides and publications. We suggest reading C. Roland Christensen and Abby J. Hansen's *Teaching and the Case Method* (1987) as a good first step. Anyone thinking about writing a case study, no matter what the length and degree of difficulty, should review this literature for suggestions and techniques.

Teaching the Case Study

The "how" of teaching a case study goes right back to its primary purpose, which is to have our students engaged in an active, enthusiastic conversation—primarily among themselves—that flows from the materials they have studied. The teacher's role is to help this conversation or discussion along by preparing the classroom setting, creating an open environment, probing for what the students think, refereeing the classroom dynamic, and overseeing how the students go about the analysis (Myers and Weeks, 1974, p. 6). Abby J. Hansen advises that the "immediate objective" for discussion leaders is to "get people to take positions and defend them." The "longer range objective" should be to raise "as many issues—central and peripheral—as possible, based on the raw data that the case provides, and send participants home pondering them" (Christensen, Hansen, and Moore, 1987, pp. 5-6).

Obviously, teachers must be well prepared before the class activity begins. This preparation breaks down into some important steps:

1. *Know the case study backward and forward:* When teaching a case study, we have to prepare in depth, with an eye to our roles as discussion leaders and to the ways our students will pursue the case. This means trying to envision how they will do this and anticipating possible reactions, snags, and opportunities. An in-depth study of any type of case we select is critical for teaching. What are its major issues and questions? Where might students get sidetracked and confused? When might it be necessary to feed in extra information or draw together loose ends in a summary?

2. *Structure the classroom environment for the best possible interaction:* This step goes back to some material we covered in Chapter Three. A good classroom setup for a case study is the U-

shape, where everyone can see and speak directly to each other. Some teachers prefer tables that seat groups of no more than five students in order to stimulate group discussions. If possible, each group should have its own flip chart and marking pens. With this equipment, the groups can prepare outlines of their cases, then tape them on the wall for presentations or comparisons. Given the need for small-group discussions, problem solving, media presentations, and other activities within the case study, the size of a class should be carefully considered to obtain the best results: too few students provide inadequate numbers for discussion; too many students present insurmountable problems in terms of meaningful participation.

3. *Review the basics of raising questions and monitoring discussions:* As anyone who has watched a first-rate discussion will attest, raising questions that will stimulate thinking and interaction among students takes some skill. Also, keeping discussion going at a high level requires some practice and self-discipline as a teacher. As discussion teachers, we are not emceeing a game show of right-and-wrong answers, nor are we trying to manipulate our students to a narrow band of correct responses. Questioning has to be open-ended, just like the case study itself. Obviously, questions come in all sizes and shapes, and it is our job to see that we use them to encourage, guide, and follow up on discussion activity. C. Roland Christensen, the dean of case study teaching, points out: "You have to create a typology of questions—challenge questions, hypothetical questions, and so on." And teachers need to figure out "when each kind of question is best employed" (Maas, 1991, p. 4). Here are some examples of different types of case study questions modeled on approaches used by leading case study teachers (Jacobson, 1984, p. 20; Christensen, Garvin, and Sweet, 1991, pp. 159–160; Christensen and Hansen, 1987; Boehrer and Linsky, 1990; Fisher, 1978):

- *Discussion starters:* "What's the dilemma that this case poses?" "How do you interpret Ms. X's actions?" "Why do you think that the Green Grass Corporation filed for bankruptcy?" "Can you help me understand what role Mr. Brown plays in this case?"
- *Probing and challenging questions:* "Can you tell me what happened as a result of that action?" "How did things get more

confused after that meeting?" "Did the president really believe that statement?" "What did the data and the statistical report suggest?"

- *Connecting questions:* "Does the decision Mr. Y made relate at all to our textbook theory on problem solving?" "Does Reynold's experience with Madelaine fit in here?" "What does the problem in this case study imply for your career?"
- *Predictive and hypothetical questions:* "Which of the applicants do you think Ms. Farnsworth ought to put on the short list?" "If the counselor had been in the principal's shoes, how would she have handled the situation?" "Imagine that a primary value for this society was competition—how would that change things in the life of the village?"
- *Analytical and evaluative questions:* "Which of the actions the secretary of state took in developing Southeast Asian policy proved most important?" "What evidence is there in the documents to indicate that Ms. N had a choice?" "Can you rank the designs based on how aesthetically compelling they are?"
- *Summary questions:* "What are the main points of this case study we've discussed so far?" "Can you summarize the decisions that the engineers made in their initial inventory?" "Which of the communication theories we've studied have been applied by Mr. Doublespeak?"

Of course, the design and delivery of questions, along with the nonverbal cues teachers give students (that infamous "body language"), make an enormous difference. Though challenging questions may be appropriate at key moments, an interrogation will probably not produce positive results for interaction. So a question like "Where did you get an idea like that?" delivered with an acid tone will only deaden classroom spirit. However, the same question, prefaced by "approving statements, delivered with a relaxed stance and in a calm, friendly tone of voice" (Christensen, Hansen, and Moore, 1987, p. 8), will create the environment for a successful case discussion.

Finally, many case studies should have study questions attached as a preliminary to the class meeting. The trick here is not to cut off discussion and new ideas by providing study questions that lead students to one point of view. Study questions should draw attention to important actions, evidence, and characters without predetermining the case's outcome. Study questions might also suggest a very loose outline of how the discussion might proceed. We say "might" because a tightly followed script will spoil the purpose of an open-ended case study and turn the whole exercise into an attempt to answer the question, "Who's got the teacher's correct answer?"

In the Classroom

The watchwords for teachers, once the classroom discussion of the case study starts, are *helping, listening,* and *monitoring.* In the matter of *helping* a class actively participate and learn through discussion, teachers who regularly use case studies suggest several techniques. Principal among these are the prediscussion study questions, in-class study groups on specific aspects of the case, and simple role plays of main characters. These techniques get students thinking and prepare them for what goes on in discussing the case study. The more we can do to get our students to identify with the case situation and its major actors, the more we will see active participation. We can help students by asking them to consider analogous situations from personal experiences and by creating situations in which they assume the roles of main characters.

   Listening is a skill that all the case study experts underline as a teaching virtue. It stands to reason that poor listeners, whether they are students or teachers, will not work together smoothly and raise discussions to a high level. Good questioning by the teacher depends on hearing correctly what students are saying and how they are reacting to the gist of the discussion. How often have we jumped on a partial phrase in a student's response to a question, merely in order to make our particular teaching point? In so doing, we may have cut off a new point of view or a future contribution by that same student. Listening more carefully can also warn us of students' frustrations and alert us to their struggles in understanding an idea within their own frame of experience. Listening alertly is perhaps the best guarantee against forgetting one's primary obligation as a discussion teacher, which is to guide with questions rather than teach in the spotlight.

Monitoring the case study discussion is more than a question of asking questions. It involves creating a relaxed environment in which all ideas are encouraged and every participant is given the opportunity to contribute. Again, the experts suggest a variety of approaches, some of which are pretty basic but all too often forgotten:

• It will take some time and effort, but we will obtain nice dividends in discussions by getting to know our students as individual learners, taking account of their strengths, weaknesses, and level of preparation; how they react to questioning; how they interact with other students; their areas of experience; and shyness, a sense of humor, and other traits related to classroom learning. Learn the students' names as quickly as possible! A good start is to use name cards that the students set in front of their place.

• Knowing when to draw the line when discussions are stuck or are wandering off on a tangent is important. We do not want to block the natural movement of a discussion or be overcontrolling, forcing our students down a narrow path with specific goals to attain. Students need a chance to investigate things on their own initiative with plenty of room for spontaneous effort. At the same time, when their enthusiasm clearly is leading them astray, we need to pose questions that guide them back to the main point.

• Involving everybody in the discussion is an interesting challenge. Some strategies for generating discussions include asking the questions the right way (such as giving an easy question to a shy student), letting students warm up in small groups, singling out others for participation in role plays, creating a teamwork approach, and appreciating all honest contributions, without penalty for their correctness, sophistication, or delivery. In this last regard, guiding the discussion contributions of some students requires wisdom and, sometimes, a saintly patience.

• We are not always dispassionate choreographers directing the action in a case study discussion. Depending on the subject and our objectives for a case study, we can help things along by sharing our thinking with students. Thus, someone teaching a case study on marketing ethics who once worked in the industry might add

important personal insights to discussions. Or students might learn
from the insights of last semester's group analysis of the same case
problem.

Teaching Tip: Case Study Pre-reports
Once again, Earl Bolick, a professor of management,
has some sage advice for teachers. Bolick has each student prepare a report on the main issues, problems,
and concerns of the assigned case study before coming
to class. In group discussions that begin the class session, the students compare their reports and attempt
to reach a consensus. As a result, they learn from each
other and begin formal discussion of the case study
with wider perspectives.

Finally, a few words about the job of concluding a case study
are in order. Just as with simulations, concluding a case study with
summarizing and debriefing is an important teaching tool. With
each case study, we can include a written section that describes how
the key actors resolved their dilemma in the actual or hypothetical
case. So, for example, in the case of Leota Shaw, we might supply
a second written narrative that describes how Jones dealt with this
student and the problem she posed for teaching his diplomatic history class. This added information provides opportunities for additional analysis and discussion as well as a chance for the class to
start wrapping things up. Once students begin *summarizing* their
conclusions, we need to be careful not to step in and give them "the
word." As experienced case study teachers warn, our authoritative
opinion at this point may backfire. Some students may ask, "Why
should I bother studying so hard?" Others may clam up in discussion "and will simply wait to be told the answer at the end of the
class, or will try to second-guess how the instructor will handle the
case" (Rich, 1969, p. 15). As bright students no doubt will protest,
a case study is supposed to be open-ended, without a right answer.
And being too heavy-handed in giving our formal opinions will
compromise that principle. At the same time, our opinions on how
the case study discussion is going are legitimate as summary mate-

rial. We can include comments, hints, connections, generalizations, commendations, and overviews at this time, so long as we do not force preconceived conclusions on students.

**Teaching Tip: Teaching Technical Subjects
with Case Studies**

Despite the case study's many advantages, according to Bruce Greenwald (1991, pp. 196–198), the teaching of technical subjects presents "special difficulties." Students' "expectations" and "anxieties" about mastering essential information and techniques in a chemistry class, for example, may conflict with a case study teaching approach that encourages exceptionally free-flowing discussion. The teaching of case studies in technical fields necessitates a highly structured approach, and "the challenge is to impose this structure in a way that does not stifle the free flow of ideas" [p. 198].

At the end of any case study, students need time for *debriefing* and *reflection,* during which they can draw generalizations about the case materials, what they have learned, and how they might apply their learning. For example, students in a counseling class might reflect on how they applied interpersonal theories and skills during a case study. Of course, we will want to include, as part of debriefing, time for students to evaluate the case study strategy and our own teaching methods, so that we can improve our approach for the next go-around.

Finally, *summarizing* is important. As Christensen urges teachers using the case study approach, right after class, "get back to the office and put down in black and white your own summary of the class discussion: What were the issues covered and ignored? What key questions remained partially considered? What are the leads for the next class?" Christensen also suggests considering the good and the bad moments during the class, perhaps developing a teaching diary for assessing ourselves and our courses so we can do a better job next time (Jacobson, 1984, p. 19). Not bad advice for any kind of teaching strategy.

Teaching Model: Evaluating Case Study Participation

Teachers new to the case study method rightfully raise questions about how they can evaluate their students. Through short written exercises and any examinations or papers, teachers will have some hard evidence with which to assign a grade. The focus here is on how well the students dealt with what the case study presents in terms of information, issues, problems, and dilemmas. But, if a teacher wishes to grade students' participation in everyday discussions accurately and fairly, how is that accomplished? Some teachers retire to their offices immediately after each class period to jot down checks or pluses on a class roll, as well as comments indicating the frequency of students' participation; the quality of their contributions, preparation, and analyses; and even their skills and behaviors as participants in a discussion setting. For purposes of comparison and to draw out differences in perception, teachers can ask students to assess their individual contributions.

Hank Tkachuk, a professor of speech and theater, has put together a means of grading student participation in his case studies that could be adapted to other situations. The chart shown in Exhibit 7.1 gives general criteria for each level of achievement so that students know what Tkachuk expects when he assesses their preparations, analyses, and contributions. As the chart reveals, he encourages student participation in this process by asking that they grade themselves on each exercise.

Final Thoughts

In summary, case studies pose a realistic problem that is "open-ended," without pat answers. Effective case studies invite analysis, discussion, reflection, and sometimes further research. They require students to decide what they would do in a given situation and to assess the results and consequences of what they have done. Because case study preparation, teaching, and follow-up demand a great

Exhibit 7.1. Case Study Grades.

Student: _____

Date	Case Name	Student Grade	Instructor Grade	Comments

Grades for case studies (instructor evaluations for each case study are based, in general, on the following criteria):

4.0 (A) Contributed frequently and appropriately; applied relevant data and theory to the problem; encouraged others to participate; "managed" the discussion appropriately; made no factual errors; built on the comments of others; made integrative statements
3.0 (B) Made no errors of fact or theory; occasionaly employed theory to explain the case; offered some new information; offered solutions but without complete explanations using theory; contributed regularly
2.0 (C) Contributed a few times; offered some new information; employed some theory, but with some errors and vagueness; made statements unconnected to main subject or repeated comments already offered
1.0 (D) Was present, but contributed minimally to case study; significantly misapplied theory and offered informative comments with factual errors; violated behavior and discussion guidelines
0.0 (F) Absent from class without excuse

deal from teachers, it is likely that most of us will not construct an entire course revolving around this active-learning strategy; yet including even a single case study activity in a semester will sharpen our teaching skills and open up the discussion for our students to participate.

PART 3

Resources
That Encourage
Active Learning

EIGHT

Integrating
Reading Materials
and Guest Speakers

Designing effective classroom strategies is only part of what it takes to create a successful active-learning environment. Without stimulating resources that help ignite our students' thinking and intellectual curiosity, our best efforts at active learning will be for naught. Obviously, we need to select resources, such as reading assignments, problem-oriented texts, other printed sources, and visits from outside experts, with an eye to encouraging students to interact and participate enthusiastically. Equally important is how well we prepare assignments and guide our students' reading, analysis, and listening. In this chapter, we will concentrate initially on ways to develop successful reading assignments and match them with active-learning strategies. Next, and probably more relevant for those who teach technical subjects where reading assignments are secondary to instructional texts, we will take a look at using campus colleagues and persons from the community as resources for active learning.

Reading Assignments and Print Sources

No matter what we ask students to read for our classes—textbooks, primary documents, newspapers, magazines, or other printed materials—we rely heavily on those texts as sources for active learning. Most of us assign hefty chunks of reading and print materials. However, we often get so busy delivering our lectures, trying to get through the syllabus, and running classroom activities that we fail to use those assigned homework readings effectively. We neglect *in class* what we have demanded that students read outside of class. As a result, students eventually conclude that the assigned readings do not count for much.

Our students' failure to do their reading usually hits home when we discover that one of our favorites—Professor Klupinski's article on jet propulsion, for example—is now just deadwood. How could the students neglect that one? A good answer, unfortunately, is that in our students' opinion few reading assignments have any real connection to classroom lectures, activities, and discussions. Or, if our lectures pretty much repeat what we are asking them to read, they conclude, and justly so, "Why read when I will hear the same thing in class?" As the semester speeds by, and tests and papers pile up, we begin to wonder, "Are the students doing any reading at all?" This gnawing question reinforces our need to spend even more time on lectures to make sure that students get the content we think they so desperately need. And the more time we spend lecturing, the less time is available for engaging students in discussion and other activities—a vicious circle indeed!

It seems clear that if we do not make special efforts to use assigned readings, we cannot expect our students to take them seriously. They will not relate them to their discussions, papers, and exams. The connection between what we ask students to read outside class and what we expect them to do in class must be strong, especially if related active-learning strategies are to succeed.

The Purpose of Reading Assignments

Why assign readings in the first place? Why not let what happens in the classroom suffice for the whole teaching and learning experience?

Presumably, we assign readings because they are an efficient way to convey information and to help students learn about our disciplinary perspectives. Readings, of course, are more central to some disciplines than to others, and readings in a math textbook are different from those in a sociology textbook. Readings can provide an overview of topics we want to cover in depth during class, or they can describe in depth the topics and issues we only have time to outline during class. They can present theory, allowing us time in class to consider examples and spell out complexities. They can be used as points of agreement and contrast. They can stretch and challenge students' thinking abilities. And they give students the chance to encounter the writings of the best minds in our disciplines.

For these reasons, reading assignments are central, not just adjunct, to our teaching efforts and classroom discussions. Students must expect that what they read makes a difference as they are learning. They must see clear connections between classroom activities, lectures, and readings. But without some help from us, students' reading efforts can go off track. So how do we keep things moving forward?

As usual, the best approach is to let students know what we are thinking and to make our expectations about reading assignments clear from the outset. Students need to know (1) what types of reading we require; (2) why the reading is important; (3) how the texts, books, and articles assigned can be read to the best advantage; and (4) how reading assignments connect to the classroom activities.

For example, at the first class meeting we might tell students something like the following, or even include it in the course syllabus:

1. *What types of reading we require:* "I'll be using Frick and Frack's *Conflicting Interpretations of World Religions.* This book is an edited collection that discusses major issues about world religions and analyzes them from two different points of view."

2. *Why the reading is important:* "I think this collection will help you understand how the experts often argue and disagree, and how their disagreements and debates can lead to new insights. You'll see as well that the subject of this course is not cut-and-dried information. As your readings will illustrate, we are not dealing with a subject that is free of bias, personal opinion, and conjecture. I also think it's important for you to experience different approaches to the subject other than what I might favor or what you might find congenial to your own point of view."

3. *How to use the readings to best advantage:* "As you read these essays, try to set the main issues and subjects of debate clearly in your mind. What differences of opinion are at stake here? Con-

centrate on general information and the gist of the arguments, because you aren't reading for facts and figures. Take notes on what you think are important ideas and issues. Compare and contrast the points of view. Look for bias and unsupported arguments. Think about where you stand in relation to the conflicting interpretations. Don't worry, I'll give you some study questions to help focus each reading assignment."

4. *How the readings connect to the classroom activities:* "And remember! The reading assignments form the basis for activities we will be pursuing in class time. For example, next week we will divide the class into debating groups. You may have to argue in favor of or against an author's view. Or you might be part of a group that does some detective work on an author's stereotypes and ethnocentrism. Each week's reading will find its way into our classroom activities."

Of course, we should do as we say. Students have taken too many courses where everything the teacher said the first day about using assigned readings turned out not to be the case. At the first opportunity, and always in connection with a class period when students have reading assignments due, we should make sure to spend time using the readings in class.

Classroom active-learning strategies should complement and build on reading assignments whenever possible. This task of connecting reading assignments to active-learning strategies can be facilitated by constructing a rough typology. Though some types probably have eluded our search, and some have limited value for teachers who are more concerned with technical content, here are suggestions for how to use reading assignments and match them to an active-learning strategy:

- *Supplemental lectures and information add-ons:* Have students take a few minutes to discuss the readings in small groups. Have a spokesperson for each group "be the teacher," to summarize, inform, or demonstrate the reading content to the class.
- *Summaries:* Give small groups a specific concept or a general school of thought discussed in the reading to outline. Have the class comment on the accuracy of these outlines as they are constructed in the small groups.

- *Primary sources:* Have students interview each other about the reading in pairs. Give them some hints about key questions to ask each other and emphasize that asking good interview questions depends on a good initial understanding of the readings.
- *Reviews:* Have students assume the roles of author and editor discussing the review's accuracy and fairness.
- *Opinion essay:* Pair students and ask them to identify any opinion statement that they agree is "true." Then have them trace the evidence, or lack of it, that the essayist uses to support the opinion (Frederick, 1989, p. 13).
- *Conflicting opinions:* Stage an in-class debate. Or the teacher can take one point of view and defend it. Ask students to raise challenges, issues, and questions based on the conflicting readings.
- *Critical analyses:* Ask students to contribute "how" and "why" questions about the reading topic for use in small-group discussions.
- *Theories and models:* Ask students to set up a role-playing situation in which the theory or model might apply.

These bridges to reading assignments make chapters, articles, and documents come alive and give them relevance for our students. The technique also makes us evaluate how good and how workable our reading assignments are. Maybe "Klupinski's article" is not as great as we thought! Putting it to an active-learning test might resolve our nagging doubts.

Guiding Students' Readings for Active Learning

Successfully linking reading assignments and classroom active-learning strategies requires that we guide students in their reading activities. As Thomas G. Devine points out, students need "to do something . . . to react [and] to respond" (Devine, 1981, p. 42) to their reading assignments if they are to take them anywhere. So study questions and reading activities are obviously a priority in most cases.

Study questions can be tricky. Questions centering on facts and those imposing a very limiting focus on the readings will not

Teaching Tip: Reading Tests

A colleague of ours requires her students to make up a test about the concepts contained in their reading assignments. She pairs up learners and they exchange the tests they have concocted. After they take each other's tests, they exchange and grade them. The students are then allowed to discuss the tests with their partners; in the process, they verify answers, question wording, and see if the tests relate enough to the reading assignment. If there are any serious disagreements during this discussion among partners, the professor acts as the arbiter. She collects all the tests and notes the grades awarded. Then she grades the tests from her perspective in relation to the quality of the questions posed.

provide a strong transition to active learning in the classroom. The idea is to focus students' attention on major concepts and issues so they will connect what they are reading to what we want to examine in class. If study questions do call for specific attention to facts, figures, and ideas, our intent should be to have students apply these elements in classroom problem solving and use them as evidence in their discussions. Therefore, we should ask our students questions that fit into prospective classroom activities, model theories and approaches used in academic disciplines and professional careers, extend meaning to materials read or discussed previously, promote a critical analysis of the materials, and make the students think about how the text applies to their personal experiences.

In providing study questions, it often makes sense to explain and emphasize certain concepts, ideas, or models that students need for successful learning. For example, a study question for a reading assignment on business management might be phrased like this:

Please take particular note of pages 13–14 of Kaisha's article in which he comments on decision making in Japanese business. Recall our discussion of decision making in the American auto industry last week. What comparisons and contrasts can you draw between the two approaches to decision making? We will be using these two approaches in a simulated decision-making exercise Thursday.

Study questions should lead students to exercise different reading and thinking skills, such as *summarizing* (arguments, issues, ideas), *identifying* (concepts, theories), *comparing and contrasting, relating* to lectures or classroom discussions, and *connecting* to personal experiences. Here are some illustrations of how study questions might be written:

1. *Summarize,* in your own words, the main point of David Mean's criticism of Andrew Lloyd Webber's production of *Phantom of the Opera.*
2. Can you *identify* two other key concepts in the reading assigned on social mobility in Singapore?
3. How would you *compare and contrast* Hawthorne's and Melville's literary use of the pastoral ideal in "Ethan Brand" and *Typee?*
4. Does the reading from May Sarton have any *relationship* to last week's discussion of individual authenticity?
5. Can you give an example from your own experience of an instance when you practiced the intervention skills the reading assignment details in relation to chemically dependent youth? (*connecting*)

In addition to study questions, Peter J. Frederick suggests that teachers can help students to read their assignments effectively by modeling how to read and interpret part of a text. An exercise of this nature can help students learn to summarize the key ideas in a reading assignment. We often forget that learning to write a simple summary involves at least basic knowledge of what is and is not important. So, for example, in a political science course, the teacher might read and highlight parts of a reading assignment showing how he goes about it. Next, the students would be asked to practice on another passage in small groups, trying to read and analyze it as if they were political scientists. Finally, the teacher can return front and center—taking up the passage the students have just completed—to once again model how analytical reading should proceed. This final step allows students some assessment of what they attempted. And, "after having struggled with a passage themselves," Frederick suggests, "hearing the teacher's interpretation has more meaning" (Frederick, 1987b, pp. 54–56).

Teaching Tip: Nonthreatening Questions
Professor H. L. Gaede asks students some informal questions about his reading assignments, such as "What of the chapter do you think we should *review?*" "What item in the chapter *surprised* you?" "What topic in the chapter can you apply to your own *experience?*" Questions such as these, Gaede suggests, will require students to do the reading, but probably "will create less tension and feelings of resistance" [Gaede, 1989, p. 4].

Here are some other techniques for engaging students in assigned readings. They can interview someone outside of the class about issues and questions raised in their reading. Instructors can design attitude and opinion surveys, based on reading assignments, that students complete outside of class (Erickson and Strommer, 1991, p. 129). And a recent technique increasingly popular with teachers is idea or concept mapping. Students are asked to picture or map out ideas and supporting evidence. The object, beyond identifying the main ideas and evidence that supports them, is to see how readings "hang together" and to graph patterns of thought and important connections (Novak and Gowin, 1984). In small groups, students can take a specific concept and construct a map of it, such as the one pictured in Figure 8.1, which maps a journal article, "Hollywood and the Cold War." Idea maps can take simple forms, such as a flowchart and a branch, or more complicated twists, depending on the students' abilities and imagination. Concept mapping, though a more complex strategy than we present here, can be adapted for small groups; it has proven value for making the

Figure 8.1. Concept Map.

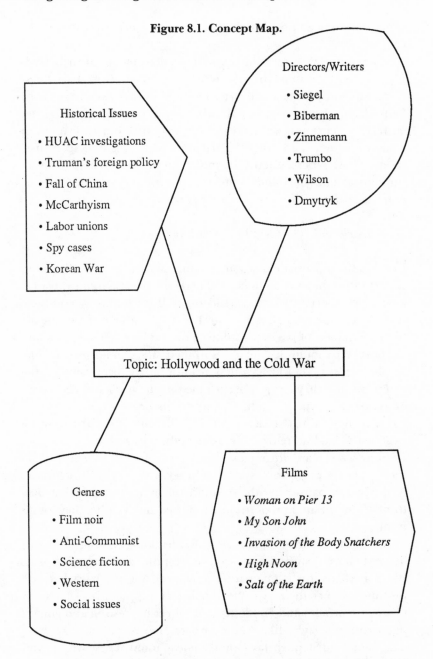

Historical Issues

• HUAC investigations

• Truman's foreign policy

• Fall of China

• McCarthyism

• Labor unions

• Spy cases

• Korean War

Directors/Writers

• Siegel

• Biberman

• Zinnemann

• Trumbo

• Wilson

• Dmytryk

Topic: Hollywood and the Cold War

Genres

• Film noir

• Anti-Communist

• Science fiction

• Western

• Social issues

Films

• *Woman on Pier 13*

• *My Son John*

• *Invasion of the Body Snatchers*

• *High Noon*

• *Salt of the Earth*

Source: Format adapted from Longman and Atkinson, 1991, p. 126.

most out of reading materials (Longman and Atkinson, 1991, chap. 4).

Finally, making students write something about their reading is important; in addition to writing out answers to study questions, student journals and brief in-class writing exercises can be helpful. Another resource we should keep in mind when designing exercises to encourage critical reading is that of our colleagues in communications and other departments where reading specialists reside. These experts usually are more than willing to help us think through assignments and to suggest models for helping students grapple meaningfully with their readings.

How Much and What Kinds of Reading?

In the active-learning classroom, reading assignments are linked to the activities students do in class. Therefore, these assignments may have to be shortened so that students will have time to complete them before the next class session. It is impossible to prescribe arbitrary numbers of pages for students to read between one class and the next. We should put ourselves in their shoes and be reasonable. Maybe students should have less reading at the beginning of the course so that they can get accustomed to the texts and classroom exercises. The type of reading assigned also makes a difference in terms of how much students can handle: obviously, they can be expected to read more pages in a novel than in a physics textbook. Keeping a scorecard during a semester on how well students handle the number of pages you assign might serve as a useful benchmark. And why not pause after the second week and ask them what they think about the amount of reading required and whether they found it interesting?

In this last regard, academic and textbook writing often can be pretty boring stuff, despite quality graphics and attractive print styles. Perhaps this is one reason why more and more teachers are putting together their own "textbooks" as supplements, made up of selected articles and handouts that reflect interesting and engaging writing. Writers like Annie Dillard, Lewis Thomas, Barbara Tuchman, and Stephen Jay Gould come to mind. These writers and others like them make reading more of a joy than a chore for our students. In certain circumstances, however, even these writers may be beyond the reading levels of many undergraduates. If this is the case, teachers will need to help direct their students' reading with study questions and other exercises as they might do with more difficult textbook readings.

Whenever possible, then, we should try to use writings that appeal to our own interests and subject needs, but that simultaneously are accessible and stimulating for students. A time-consuming and comprehensive literature search is not always necessary. However, this means paying more attention to specialty magazines and journals written for the public that often attract writers of the quality of Dillard or Gould, such as *Scientific American, Harper's,* or *American Heritage.* After all, why should we subject our students to boring and sometimes convoluted reading, when with a little effort, we can find materials that excite them as well as us.

Using Outside Resource Persons

For the most part, we go it alone in the classroom. Rarely do we invite colleagues and experts from the community to join us and share their talents, expertise, insights, and experience with our students. But we should. Someone in the local community may have that real-world experience and credibility we often lack. A colleague may have some special expertise or some research-in-progress on a topic that students should hear. Using outside resource persons may very well lead to stimulating discussions and enliven other classroom activities.

We are not so foolish as to suggest that using practitioners and colleagues is without pitfalls and risks. Despite our best efforts to choose competent resource people, in the words of Robert Burns, our "best laid schemes . . . gang aft a-gley." Many of us have survived worst-case scenarios in which visitors have bored students to death with interminable stories unrelated to course objectives, rolled in the soapbox to trumpet their favorite cause, or sometimes failed even to show up, leaving us holding the bag and wishing we had never sent an invitation in the first place. All it takes are one or two disasters like these for us to question any future visits by promising pundits.

But setting our worst fears aside, we know how exciting the special gifts and interests of invited guests can be for students. They bring an authenticity and a credibility to subjects that students seldom find in their textbooks. When presented with an insider's view on a subject, students need little encouragement to ask how theories translate into action and what it is like outside the campus walls and towers. Of course, no textbook can duplicate what the research scientist, the community organizer, the artist, the politician, the corporate executive, and even the former student can demonstrate in terms of knowledge, skills, and experiences. Using resource persons has another benefit as well, directly related to our teaching: they allow us the luxury of observing students as they learn from someone else. In the process, we can gain new perspectives on what works and what does not when it comes to getting students involved in their learning.

Teaching Tip: Finding Outside Resource Persons
One way to locate outstanding guests for classroom presentations is to check on speakers' bureau listings for community organizations, businesses, and governmental agencies. Also, most colleges and universities maintain a list of presenters. If yours does not, continuing education programs are usually chock-full of interesting courses taught by experts on particular and unusual subjects. Some areas have open universities, community continuing education bulletins, and neighborhood newsletters that feature potential guest presenters. And sometimes a visiting lecturer or consultant to the community or college can make time for special classroom visits.

Making the best use of resource people and ensuring that their visits are opportunities for active learning requires some forethought and planning. To write this chapter, we have scoured what little literature exists and solicited tips from faculty who regularly use outside resource people in their classes. This exercise provided some commonsense advice as well as the following general categories around which to organize our discussion: (1) what an outside resource person can do, (2) preparing a resource person for the class meeting, (3) preparing students for the resource person, and (4) debriefing students after the presentation.

What an Outside Resource Person Can Do

A good resource person can accomplish a number of things for our classes by:

- Clarifying areas of knowledge and expertise that we lack
- Introducing a teaching style different from our own
- Providing and discussing materials, artifacts, and research that are otherwise inaccessible
- Offering a different viewpoint—disciplinary, cultural, gender-related, and so on—on an issue within a discipline or topic of discussion
- Serving as an expert or an eyewitness for students to interview

Preparing the Resource Person for the Class Meeting

Once we have set the goals we hope to achieve, the next step is to invite the right person as a resource guest. One of the simplest yet most worthwhile bits of advice is to "choose nice people" (Cloud and Sweeny, 1988). In most cases, this means inviting someone we know personally, who shares some of our views about the goals of teaching. Or we might get a lead on a good resource person from a colleague we respect. Taking these approaches makes more sense than simply buying "a pig in a poke," although what is in the poke might be a prized expert. Yet even if a competent resource person is available, don't necessarily expect that the first visit will be without a few snags.

Some basic tips apply to using resource persons in the classroom:

- Send a confirming letter or make a phone call to the resource person about things like the class time, location, and room number.

- Think about enclosing parking passes and campus maps if necessary.
- Include a copy of your syllabus, indicating where the guest fits in and what the students have read in preparation for the classroom visit.
- Let the resource person know exactly what is expected during the visit—staging an experiment, demonstrating a technique, telling a story, fielding interview questions—and how much class time is available.
- Find out about any preferences your resource person has for an introduction, classroom seating arrangements, or audiovisual equipment.
- Encourage any guest to bring a few props to pass around for students to handle.
- Make it clear that you will be in class ready to help out and keep things on track if necessary.

Preparing Students for the Resource Person

To prevent classroom visits from turning into just another lecture, inform students that they have a responsibility to help orchestrate this session. Then coach them on how to do it. As a start, students will need to do some assigned readings—if possible, something the invited guest has written. A week before the visit, all students should be encouraged to submit a few questions they would like to ask, based on what they have read. The students can then structure a set of interview questions that will help ensure that some of the original objectives for the visit will be addressed. Perhaps the class will wish to choose a panel of students to select and ask the questions. When the resource person arrives in class, the teacher can make the introductions and turn things over to the students' panel. Following this more or less structured interview, we can open up the floor to other students for a give-and-take discussion.

Debriefing Students After the Presentation

If time allows, schedule a short debriefing session immediately after the presentation. Or set aside ten minutes or so in the next class for the same task, which may be the best alternative because the students will have had time to reflect on the session. Debriefing is a form of critical reflection, in which students think about what happened during a learning experience, consider its significance, and tie its implications to classroom concepts and issues.

Before moving forward to the next classroom topic, ask the students to pause and think quietly about the visit. You might structure this reflection by posing a few simple questions: "What stands out most in your minds about the visit?" "Did you learn anything that you didn't expect to?" "Did you have any questions you wished to ask and did not?" "What connections, correlations, and conflicts do you see between what the guest presented and the assigned readings?"

Teachers also might wish to tell students some of their reactions, whether the visit met their objectives or not, and how the issues raised might lead the students into new areas of learning.

Teaching Model: Reading and
Discussing Primary Documents

Most of the students in Thomas B. Jones's "U.S. History Since World War II" class are unfamiliar and ill at ease working with primary historical sources. They have difficulty dealing with reading assignments outside of class that feature primary sources. As one of the first units in his course, Jones introduces students to the task of reading primary sources and applying them to historical interpretation.

Following the first class, students are assigned five primary historical documents related to a specific historical issue, such as a congressional resolution, private correspondence, a memoir selection, a newspaper story, and a government agency report. The reading assignment also includes essays by historians about the issue *in which they use the documents as evidence.* Jones prepares study questions for each document and the historians' essays. He reminds students that the historians have used the primary sources in their analysis. The students are then informed that at the next class meeting, they will be discussing the readings and will be problem solving in small groups.

At the next class meeting, the twenty-five students are divided into five small groups. Each group discusses a different document. During the first ten minutes, groups are instructed to piece together a straightforward summary of what their document says. One student acts as a recorder. After the ten minutes are up, each group has five minutes to read their summary and answer questions (or receive comments) from their classmates. This reporting, questioning, and commenting gives students an opportunity to see how well they have understood the documents. It also allows each group to identify possible connections among the documents.

The groups reassemble and then discuss how the historians have used the documents in their writings. Groups focus on the context in which the document is used, how it is used as evidence for an interpretation, the accuracy of its use, and whether the historian may have missed an opportunity to see things in a different light. Each group reports its findings again, and a general discussion of the documents and the essays takes place, often with little or no prompting.

Such an exercise has considerable advantages for those teaching subjects that demand substantial reading and use difficult sources. Students begin to understand what it is like to be a professional historian and how a careful consideration of evidence is necessary to write history. Jones's experience is that when primary sources are part of reading collections (whether they are included in a general textbook, a selection of supplementary readings, or a collection duplicated by the teacher), particularly in subjects such as history, sociology, political science, and the like, students treat them like long quotes in an essay: they ignore them! But when students work in class with sources, dividing up the load and forming into small discussion groups, good things start to happen.

Teaching Model: Using Resource Persons in Philosophy

Chet Meyers uses a variety of guest speakers in his philosophy class, "Views of Human Nature in Western Culture." During the first five weeks of the quarter, students become familiar with five issues central to discussions about human nature: (1) free will and determinism, (2) learned and innate behavior, (3) good and evil, (4) mind and body, and (5) spirit and matter. Beginning with the sixth week, guest speakers present their own perspective on human nature. Meyers draws on colleagues at his own university and community resource persons who come highly recommended. Past speakers have included a Lakota spiritual leader, a Christian Science practitioner, a feminist head of a women's counseling service, and a William Blake scholar.

Meyers prepares his guest speakers by first calling them and telling them a little about the class. In particular, he discusses the five philosophical issues and lets the presenter know what students will have talked about the week prior to the visit. He also asks his guests to suggest readings and specific study questions for students to do in preparation for the visit. If the resource person has no suggested readings in mind, Meyers offers some he has used in past classes. He then mails the resource person a syllabus, the readings and study questions, and a copy of the five key philosophical issues, spelled out in depth. Prior to the visit, students are given assigned readings and study questions. They are also instructed to think about specific questions they might want to ask the resource person.

The class is taught in a three-hour format, so Meyers has the guest present for the first half of the class. Forty minutes is given to the presentation and discussion; thirty minutes is allowed for specific student questions. Then the class takes a break and the guest leaves. When the class reconvenes for the final hour and a half, Meyers asks his students how they reacted to the presentation and what they learned from it. He also tries to tie issues the guest may have introduced to concepts previously presented in class.

Meyers feels the success of these presentations hinges on two important factors: (1) using a resource person who has a track record as both a presenter and a discussion leader, and (2) actively involving the guest in the selection of readings and study questions.

Final Thoughts

Well-designed strategies and good resources are an important combination for successfully creating an active-learning environment. Reading assignments, of course, are fundamental in most college teaching and especially in active learning. Whenever possible, classroom strategies should be matched to the types of readings we assign. Active-learning strategies should be prefaced by preparing students to read effectively. The fact is that many students lack basic reading comprehension skills, such as identifying, summarizing, and contrasting. Therefore, teachers may have to review these skills, particularly in the first two weeks of class. One significant step toward that goal is to have good study questions ready. Of course, just like readings, using outside resource persons requires forethought and work in preparing students, especially if the occasion is to be worth the effort necessary to contact someone and schedule all the details. And visiting colleagues or community experts need to be readied for their roles as well. When teachers take the time necessary to prepare both their students and the visiting expert, genuine interaction and meaningful dialogue will follow.

NINE

Using Technology
Effectively

Most teachers are comfortable with the basics—textbooks, lecture notes, blackboards, and chalk—so that introducing teaching technology into our classrooms makes us a bit uneasy. Maybe we worry about looking frantic and foolish in front of our students as we search vainly for an isolated segment in a videotape. Perhaps we shy away from using some advanced technologies, such as computers, because our students may know more about them than we do. Probably, as creatures of habit, we just find it easier to stay with the tried and true, rather than experiment with an electronic presentation. Still, the educational potential inherent in technology, from creative uses of basic audiovisual equipment to more sophisticated high-tech options, is impressive, and we would be foolish to dismiss it.

In this chapter, we primarily want to consider the simple, realistic, and practical uses of technology that the majority of teachers can adapt to active-learning strategies. We cannot offer an exhaustive commentary about all the possibilities available for incorporating this technology into your teaching. Anyone who has struggled through an operating manual for a computer or videocassette recorder (VCR) will understand why we have omitted technical explanations about how something works and how to operate it. We also realize that many of our institutions do not have the resources to purchase all the technology available, particularly the newest advances on the market. Finally, the majority of us simply do not have the time necessary to explore and understand each and every possibility. And judging by the new-products sections of educational journals and computer magazines, keeping up-to-date is tough even for the most technologically literate among us. Given these realities, we will consider the pros and cons of basic media technologies that the majority of us have close at hand and can easily put to use. Then we will briefly mention some possibilities for computers and multimedia. Because our focus is on active learning, we will aim our commentary at ways *to teach actively* using technology.

Approaching Technology for Teaching

The advocates of technology enthusiastically advocate its many advantages for the teaching enterprise. We too are excited about its possibilities for the classroom. A documentary film can bring students into contact with experts and new ideas; it can re-create experiences and conditions that the best lectures and readings cannot. A multimedia videodisc offers exciting, far-reaching sources for learning at the touch of a finger. A classroom slide-tape presentation can give students access to materials that ordinarily are inaccessible or might require a costly field trip. But for each of these examples, the question must be asked: "How does this teaching technology promote active learning?"

The wonders of technology and the fact that our students may welcome its use in our classrooms do not necessarily add up to active learning. Supplying information—at the lecturer's podium or on the TV monitor—no matter how exciting, does not always stimulate students' learning. However, research, experience, and common sense do indicate that technology can be a valuable partner for teachers and learners. The key is to consider the various possibilities in a proper relationship to teaching goals, not just as devices to supply information to students. For teaching technology to reinforce our active-learning goals, it must trigger classroom activities and expand students' learning capabilities.

Regrettably, many teachers use technology primarily as filler for lectures, without much forethought as to how students actually would benefit from its application. It is comforting, of course, to shorten our teaching preparation time, knowing that a videotape will carry most of the teaching load in a class session. But if, in the process, our students doze off, we have gained nothing. With a little preparation and follow-up, such as a good set of study questions and small-group discussion, the same videotape can enhance student learning, rather than merely replacing a lecture with a videotape. In each of the sections that follow, we will share specific techniques that help increase the odds that active learning ensues when we apply teaching technology. But for now, here are a few questions to consider when thinking about using teaching technology in the classroom:

- Is the technology appropriate and the best strategy to stimulate class activities? For example, would assigned readings and a role play be better options?
- What is the purpose of using overhead transparencies? to reinforce a concept presented in the last class? to introduce something new? to challenge students' assumptions?
- What should be done before using a film to prepare students so that they will get the most out of it? develop study questions? write a brief summary of the film plot? assign some articles on theory?
- Should there be a follow-up writing assignment or a small-group discussion so that students can reflect on what they have just observed?
- How should the effectiveness of this particular technology and materials be evaluated? through a questionnaire? a short quiz? small-group discussion and reporting?

Some Theoretical Grounding for
Using Teaching Technology

Most of the literature on teaching technology deals with the mechanical aspects of its use, arguments about its effects on society (especially on children watching TV), and studies that compare it with traditional teaching in terms of testing students for recall. Not much is available on ways to combine technology with active learning. Nevertheless, we see some obvious connections between what educational researchers are discovering about learning styles and appropriate uses of technology.

One of the great advantages of teaching technology, from the overhead projector to computer graphics, is its rich capability for visual representation. The value of visual representations is heightened in the context of a growing body of research on human learning styles. We know that any group of students represents a variety of learning styles, and research has demonstrated that some learners are acutely sensitive to the power of visualization (Kleinfeld, 1972). While most of us have learned primarily by reading and listening, let us not forget that as children we had a natural attraction to visual cues and pictorial forms of learning. Many adults retain that sensitivity to visual representations. Researcher John Bransford, citing the work of Paivio, tells us that "pictures are better remembered than words, and words that can be imagined are easier to retain than less imaginable words. Imagery therefore seems to have powerful effects in learning and retention tasks" (Bransford, 1979, p. 190).

In *Teaching Students to Think Critically,* Meyers cites the value of visual representations for communicating to students a teacher's concept of critical thinking (Meyers, 1986). Diagrams that can be programmed into computer software or thrown on an overhead screen for all to see can provide efficient ways to encapsulate some of our teaching goals, such as how components of a course fit together, the steps in a problem-solving methodology, and key themes in an assigned reading. What Jill Larkin and Herbert A. Simon call "diagrammatic representations" also carry implicit information about a given process that saves time and energy in contrast to communicating the same message by a verbal sequence of propositions (Larkin and Simon, 1987). In addition to *static* representations—for example, diagrams and charts—videotapes, computer simulations, and other multimedia representations "offer a more effective way of communicating *dynamic* [italics added] concepts that change rapidly over time and space" (Lynch, 1992, p. 22). In disciplines that deal with dynamic concepts—engineering students, for instance, might use a computer simulation of changes in structural design—teaching technology clearly has the edge over static printed representations in textbooks or on handouts.

The value of visual representations such as films, pictorials, and diagrams as a means of communication in teaching goes beyond mere efficiency. In the context of active learning, visualizations can provide opportunities for students to process and ponder information when we allow them time to draw their own conclusions before we offer ours. Thus, in using any form of technology for teaching, we need to allow time for students to absorb, incorporate, and reflect on the information they are receiving. The point here is that because we know that students learn in different ways, teaching technology represents an opportunity to enhance and reinforce these different learning styles, as well as to challenge students to try different approaches to learning.

Let us now examine some ways in which we can best use technology to foster an active-learning environment in our classrooms. We will do so by considering some relatively familiar and simple kinds of technology all teachers are likely to have at hand: (1) overhead and slide projectors, (2) films, videotapes, and commercial and educational television programming, and (3) videocassette cameras. We will also look briefly at more sophisticated options, just to alert our readers to some exciting technology they might want to consider.

Overhead and Slide Projectors

The overhead projector's simplicity of operation belies its versatility and value as a teaching tool. A great advantage of transparencies, especially with recent technology, is that they can reproduce just about anything a regular photocopier can—even colors are a possibility. The overhead shines no better than in math, science, and statistics courses where graphs, charts, and problem solving are central to the learning process. The cost of creating transparencies of such textbook material is minimal, and teachers can avoid holding up their text and pointing to a diminutive graph or table while students frantically crane their necks and ask, "What page is it on?"

Teachers can use transparencies and a transparency pen to help students work through the steps of most problem-solving exercises. Active learning takes place as students are asked to supply the steps they took in problem solving. Errors are easily wiped clean as teacher and students work together to discover the best solution. Teachers also gain valuable insights about common errors often made by their students in such an approach to a problem-solving exercise.

In using transparencies or slides to illustrate presentations, some practical considerations come to mind. We recently attended a critical-thinking conference where the featured presenter relied heavily on transparencies to illustrate his talk. But the audience quickly got lost trying to stay with him. His delivery was not the problem. Indeed, he was most engaging, almost charismatic. As he bounded along, merrily flipping transparencies on the screen in rapid-fire succession, his audience got lost trying to copy down the important information on the transparencies. In terms of active learning, no one had time to *reflect* on what the presenter said, let alone copy down important points of information. As a net effect, the transparencies ended up detracting from a potentially exciting presentation. Obviously, students in classrooms can experience the same frustration.

Anyone who decides to use overhead transparencies also should make an identical set of handouts for students before the class begins. The students can then pay attention to the instructor, ask questions, and make notes on their copies of the handouts. They will be listening and working with the materials, rather than madly copying them down. The amount of information on a transparency should be kept to three or four main points. Remember, the purpose for using transparencies is to illustrate and emphasize what students are learning. As with most classroom use of media, make sure students have enough light to take notes.

Much of what we have said about using overheads applies to slides, with the exception that slides are somewhat more expensive and time-consuming to create. Many educational companies cater to teachers and have fine sets of slides for illustrating topics in biology, botany, geology, astronomy, and the other sciences, as well as the applied arts. Once again, though, showing slides does not guarantee active learning. The point is to create ways that students can get involved with the material as you are illustrating it.

Films, Videocassettes, and Commercial
and Educational Television

The VCR and its predecessor, the sixteen-millimeter projector, open up a number of attractive possibilities for active learning. What is available on film and videocassette includes a staggering array of feature films, documentaries, and presentations designed specifically for the classroom. Many colleges and universities have their own libraries of films and videocassettes, but often resources are limited. Some public libraries carry materials at reasonable rental fees. In larger metropolitan areas, the collections in public libraries can be quite extensive. Then, of course, there are video stores, mail-order catalogs with items to rent and purchase, and other colleges and universities from which to borrow. Sometimes it is advantageous to tape snippets from television broadcasts for the classroom. When using this videotaped material, be sure to follow the copyright and viewing restrictions that apply. The Public Broadcasting System makes most of its television presentations available for off-screen taping and for rental and purchase. It makes good sense to get on their mailing list (1320 Braddock Place, Alexandria, Virginia, 22314-1698) and the lists of other major distributors of films and videotapes.

The advantage of using a VCR instead of the sixteen-millimeter projector is that a videotape has more versatility as a teaching tool. Teachers can use the remote control to quickly isolate segments of a videotape presentation for viewing and reviewing. Some teachers ask questions and insert their own comments at appropriate points by stopping the videotape. If editing equipment is available, sections of various videotapes can be copied and collected on a single tape—a great time-saving device. Because most students have access to VCRs and television broadcasts, teachers can save time for more intensive viewing and discussion in the classroom by assigning an entire motion picture or documentary for viewing outside the class. Students can work in teams outside of class to study and prepare an in-class discussion of a particular topic, theme, or issue.

Teaching Tip: Digital Counting on the VCR

Nothing is more frustrating for a room of students than to have the professor struggling amateurishly to find that "really interesting" section on the tape. The digital counter found on most VCRs helps us note exactly where to start, stop, and fast-forward a videotape. When previewing a tape before showing it in class, use the digital counter and write down the numbers for the best parts of the tape you will use. Students will appreciate the extra time you have taken to make things run smoothly. But remember, digital counters vary from one brand of videotape machine to another! Preview the tape on the machine you plan to use in class.

The attractiveness of films and videocassettes is powerful. Who can resist inviting nationally known experts and commentators into the classroom to stimulate students' interests? But if intellectual stimulation is the goal, we must sometimes save students from themselves by keeping them from slipping into that vegetative stupor they all too often assume in front of a television screen. We need to use films and videotapes as active-learning teaching tools, and that means interrupting the flow of drama sometimes to help students ponder and then practice the analytical skills we are trying to teach.

At our university, a number of faculty use the feature film *Educating Rita* in an introductory educational planning class. Most students find the film engaging—almost too engaging. To make the film an active-learning experience, students are given study questions before the videotape begins—for example: "What barriers did Rita confront in pursuing her education?" "What internal and external resources did she draw on to continue her pursuit?" "How does Rita change as she becomes more involved in her education?" Then, at several key points in the film, the tape is stopped, the lights are turned on, and students work in small groups to address the study questions and reflect on the relationship between the main characters. Although the start-and-stop study-question approach is disconcerting for those who want to watch the film as pure entertainment, it is effective for critical-thinking exercises that focus on issues of educational planning. Also, with this classroom technique, teachers are not faced with a room full of students lost in reverie and intellectually disengaged when the film ends.

In the matter of commercial television programming, whether assigned for viewing out of class or videotaped for use in class, we admit that such material presents a potential mine field. Given the moronic content of most commercial broadcasting, adding to the number of hours students have already logged at their television sets is a moral issue for some of us. Even so, by having students watch specific programs, teachers can use the worst of the "boob tube" as working material for developing critical thinking and viewing skills—for example, identifying sexist stereotyping in situation comedies, examining values reflected by MTV or Saturday-morning cartoons for kids, and weighing the impact of commercials on the televising of actual events, such as news specials and political interviews.

One example of the use of commercial broadcasting illustrates how we can teach students to be critical viewers. A political science professor has her students watch news reports and interviews that deal with political figures and public policy issues. Before they do this, she gives them a short course about the camera use, interviewing techniques, and editing that are typical of such programming. (Her students are always interested to learn about the heavy and subjective editing of interviews.) She also gives students a set of general questions to encourage critical viewing—for example: How does the news program start? Is the emphasis on two conflicting points of view? Are there other political viewpoints represented? How much time is the interviewee allowed to develop an idea? She also reminds students to observe how sound and image are used as emotional and symbolic tools. Students then are prepared to discuss and analyze what they have seen. Experts have written extensively and from a variety of disciplinary angles about critical viewing. Using these expert commentaries as a guide, teachers can prepare their students well for watching television broadcasts, as well as motion pictures and documentary productions (Brookfield, 1986; Hefzallah, 1987; Salomon, 1979; O'Connor, 1987).

Since the advent of cable systems, television has offered expanded educational opportunities. In many communities, even in the dorms, students might select from a number of cable channels to watch a science class sponsored by another university, a foreign-language program, an interview of local political experts, or a hard-to-find silent movie. Teachers can keep an eye on what will be aired on local television and cable by scanning the various weekly program guides, or they can call local channels to inquire when a special program will be shown and possibly repeated. By turning our students' attention to selected programming such as that offered through public television, we can direct them to first-rate documentaries, debates, educational programs, news specials, motion pictures, and dramatizations that can serve as the starting point for in-class exercises and discussions.

Here are a few remaining tips on the use of films and videotapes. Be sure to preview a film before showing it to a class. Think about how the material can lend itself to active learning. Remember that films or videotapes are still "texts" with specific content. Consider if the presentation is appropriate to the students' level of learning in a subject. And, equally important, ask whether it speaks to students' life experiences, because some of us in the "aging professoriate" need to realize that films or videotapes we find well suited to our teaching goals may be dated, making reference to events and experiences that younger students cannot easily appreciate.

Videocassette Cameras

Today's videocassette cameras are quite portable and easy to operate. Fortunately, one does not have to be extremely knowledgeable and artistic to get a clear picture and reasonable sound. Local booksellers and libraries are stocked with simple and well-illustrated booklets on how to use a videocassette camera, edit, and record sound. The video camera is well suited to cooperative-learning projects and role plays. By wielding video cameras, students can exercise their creative talents to better understand, analyze, and discuss subjects. For example, students in a sociology class might do some background reading, research, and discussion on conformity and individualism as conflicting cultural values. Then they could create a brief videocassette presentation of examples drawn from campus life and could present the video for analysis and discussion by the class. During a class dealing with gender and language, students could videotape a role play about a female supervisor and her male employee. The class would then review the videotape immediately, discussing the concepts and issues that emerge. The teacher can stop the videotape at key points and participants can recall instantly what they were thinking and feeling (Kagan, 1984, p. 93).

In the sciences, students in a biology class could study a local bird species and produce a documentary of sorts on life cycle and local habitat. The very process of planning, recording, and editing involved in this activity sets students to cooperative tasks with all the benefits associated with that active-learning strategy. If a class has access to video cameras, videotapes are cheap and the technology is simple enough to use without much fuss. Of course, any editing by students of their videotapes would require some technological savvy on their part or some help from campus experts. Then, again, they might negotiate some assistance from fellow students in media who know the ins and outs of editing. Creative teachers have combined the resources of different classes to create cross-disciplinary collaborative projects.

Microcomputers and Other High-Tech Options

Allow us to turn conventional wisdom on its head and start this section with some caveats. Why? Because what we want to discuss about microcomputers and other technology for active learning must first emphasize the debit side of the ledger for the average teacher. While advocates will say that working with this technology is not solely the expert's province, such assessments are hard to accept. Our impression is that most college teachers share the same boat with us; we are struggling to work our word-processing programs without calamity! We assume that many readers will be novices in terms of learning how these high-tech options work. In addition, using computer approaches and other technology is expensive and takes a lot of time to develop for the classroom.

Before striding boldly into the high-tech arena, teachers should follow these steps:

1.   Discover what resources and consulting experts are available. Does the college have a media center? Do media center personnel have the time to teach some basics about the technology and its use? What about colleagues and off-campus experts? Can they help? Are other instructors and departments using similar technology and approaches? Will they share information and equipment?
2.   Find out if the necessary equipment, such as computer terminals or media stations, is available and convenient for use in a classroom or media center.
3.   Determine if enough time is available to learn about the technology, practice its use, and develop applications for active-learning strategies.

If such a check on help, equipment, and personal time is generally positive, then using some of the technology described in the remainder of this section is a possibility.

In Chapter Six, we touched on the role computers can play in simulations. Computer-based simulation exercises and games allow students to solve problems and experience situations that the computer technology can present with great detail and extensive data bases. Also, computer simulations in the sciences offer alternatives to expensive and often dangerous lab experiments. For example, one available program simulates surgery for medical students who can scalpel through any layer of a computer cadaver. In other subjects, students can play computer-simulation games that put them into real-world environments that would be difficult to experience firsthand. For example, classes dealing with legal or ethical issues can use programs that simulate courtroom trials and presentation of evidence.

Students using computer simulations are hardly passive objects in the learning process; they must manipulate the software and solve the problems it poses. But our interest in active learning is on having students interact with each other, not just their machines. Fortunately, most of the computer-simulation exercises and games allow for active learning. For example, students can work together in twos or threes at a computer without undue difficulty. Or some teachers might cluster two or more computers throughout the classroom so that students can share their observations with each other as they work through a simulation or other exercises. For those with the right equipment or access to a specially designed computer classroom, interaction is possible through a network in which students at individual terminals can share computer files and communicate back and forth electronically. They can also network to collaborate on writing assignments. Using a liquid-crystal display (LCD), teachers can project the contents of a computer screen on a classroom wall so that a larger group of students can discuss information and work together on problems.

A closely related, emerging technology relying on computers is multimedia. Back in the 1960s, multimedia meant combining into one presentation—usually on multiple screens—slides, film clips, audiotaped music, and narration. But technology has transformed multimedia into a new dimension for education. Now, according to the multimedia mavens, we think in terms of "student stations that house computer software programs" for controlling "the display of motion video, still images, and sound from a videodisc and/or videotape player, a CD-ROM drive, or other digital storage device" (Jones and Smith, 1992, p. 39). Multimedia is sort of a souped-up version of what a computer can present for instruction, incorporating a broader range and better quality of sound, motion, and image. Of course, what appears on the monitor can always be projected as a larger image with the LCD. As we write this section, one computer software manufacturer has developed a package that does not need a separate videodisc player or VCR and monitor. This is a good example of how fast the technology is changing, and why the average faculty member usually needs to find expert assistance.

How does multimedia technology encourage active learning? In this "star wars" branch of teaching technology, small groups of students can work together at their "stations," concentrating on simulations and cooperative exercises; they may even modify the software and construct their own materials. Recent periodicals are filled with interesting examples of electronic-teaching technology. At the University of Pennsylvania, students use videodisc technology to help

learn a foreign language. Two or three students gather at worksta-
tions to watch a foreign film, such as *La Strada*. The top three-fourths
of the screen on the monitor is allowed for the film; the bottom
quarter contains "windows" that students manipulate to receive commentary, translations, movie reviews, and other information about *La
Strada* ("Interactive Videodisks . . . ," 1991, pp. A18–A20).

With most high-tech options, the teaching techniques we
have described as part of other active-learning strategies—such as
small-groups and simulations—would apply. Students will require
some guidelines for working together at a multimedia workstation,
and they will need to have some time for debriefing after tackling
a computer-based simulation. We would hazard a guess that students will profit greatly from any teacher's advice that directs them
toward interaction with one another as a condition of learning with
this advanced technology. Kozma and Johnston (1991, p. 19) think
that the new teaching technology gives students "a more active role
in constructing knowledge, with an implicit change in the role of
the teacher." Therefore, they suggest that the teacher will need to
be more of a "coach or mentor, helping students solve problems
presented by the software."

Final Thoughts

Teaching successfully with technology, whether we are using overhead projectors, VCRs, or microcomputers, depends both on the
quality of instructional material we select and on the classroom
strategies we design. The timeworn slogan "garbage in, garbage
out" only describes part of the learning equation as far as we are
concerned. For example, the best software package for a computer
still has the power to isolate one student from another's ideas, suggestions, and cooperation. We repeat our earlier appeal for teaching
technology to be viewed in "a proper relationship to teaching goals,
not just as devices to supply information to students."

On the other hand, we encourage you (and ourselves) to explore the possibilities. At least pay a visit to the campus media
center and consider some of the exciting potential these teaching
technologies can add to an active-learning classroom.

TEN

Developing and Assessing Instructional Expertise

The case we have made for active learning is built on two basic assumptions: (1) that learning is by nature an active enterprise and (2) that individuals learn in different ways. The validity of these assumptions is well supported by the available research on teaching and learning. Along the way, we have also incorporated pedagogical assumptions gleaned from acknowledged classics of educational thought and from contemporary educators whose work we greatly respect. However, as we argued in favor of using active-learning strategies, we always came back to the two assumptions that originally guided our thinking. For, if learning is active and people learn in different ways, then teachers who rely solely on any one approach to teaching will miss connecting effectively with large numbers of their students.

But good teachers need not become active-learning chameleons, adept at quickly and naturally changing their teaching styles and values to fit each new teaching situation. We will not be good teachers by using approaches that make us uncomfortable, and we cannot hope to be expert at all the strategies spelled out in this book. At the same time, many of us do need to expand our teaching skills. In doing so, we can meet students on their own turf and stretch their ability to approach learning in different ways, all of which seems vital as our student bodies grow in diversity.

Another reason we advocate active learning has to do with what we see as the larger aims of education. By providing opportunities to practice active-learning strategies, we hope students will become self-directed and collaborative, critically reflective, politically savvy, empathic, and fair-minded, as well as competent in the skills that are essential to meaningful lives and careers. We think that such students will help make our society more democratic and a better place for everyone. This may sound like a rather grandiose set of expectations to lay at the door of active learning. But teachers are in a unique position to create a ripple effect from the small things we do in a classroom—assuming we know what we are about. Teaching is a vocation that asks of teachers some vision of what they hope to accomplish. "Teaching," as Stephen Brookfield tells us, "is about making some kind of dent in the world so the world is different than it was before you practiced your craft. Knowing clearly what kind of dent you want to make in the world means you must continually ask yourself the most fundamental evaluative question of all—What effect am I having on students and their learning?" (Brookfield, 1990, pp. 18–19).

The kind of dent we want to make is to help our students gain more control over their lives, but more than that, we want to support them in challenging the conventional wisdom of our culture and, in particular, to challenge assumptions they hold uncritically that might contribute to our present political, economic, and ecological crises. Some may say that this is not a task for educators. We disagree. It comes with the territory, whether we admit to it or not. We prefer to acknowledge the reality of the task and to give our students the chance, in a paraphrase of John Winthrop's words, "to do right in a world that does wrong." Because active-learning strategies require more self-direction, collaboration, empathy, listening, clarity of thought, and application of theory to practice, we believe that the active-learning classroom is a strong crucible for responsible citizenship in the broadest sense of the word.

Active-learning strategies help students connect what they are studying to their personal lives. Teachers who employ active learning are not giving students disembodied facts, figures, theories, and methodologies, but are sharing the practical ways historians, physicists, philosophers, nurses, and social scientists go about working in their disciplines. Ideas and theories come alive as students and teachers struggle to see the practical implications of academic disciplines through small-group discussions, case studies, simulations, and cooperative projects. Teachers who see themselves less as purveyors of the truth and more as "midwife" teachers encourage students to explore the practical dimensions of a subject, thus making it more relevant to their daily lives. By our deemphasizing the teacher's role as an authority figure, as active learning certainly demands, the tone of classroom learning changes and students develop their own voice (Belenky, Clinchy, Goldberger, and Tarule, 1986).

Active-learning strategies also hone the understandings and skills that a college education tries to supply. In their careers, students will draw much from their overall experiences in active-learning classrooms. They will also complete their college study with more competence in the areas of liberal learning that our college catalogs so often trumpet. Their skills and abilities in critical thinking, problem solving, reflecting, blending cognitive and affective responses, and working collaboratively will endure long beyond their memory of the chemical formula for sulfuric acid or the shape of a Doric column.

Finally, by adapting an active-learning methodology, teachers address one of the most problematic aspects of education—that of motivation. Years ago, Alfred North Whitehead commented: "There can be no mental development without interest. . . . You may endeavor to excite interest by means of birch rods, or you may coax it by the incitement of pleasurable activity. But without interest there will be no progress" (Whitehead, [1929] 1967, p. 31). Many of us have tried "birch rods," only to discover their limitations. Our own experience with using active-learning strategies is that students do indeed find them interesting, and often pleasurable. And our students' improved motivation, as a result of this increased interest, has made their learning more meaningful and our teaching more enjoyable.

How Teachers Can Change

As we have implied throughout this book, an active-learning approach to teaching only succeeds to the degree that teachers are willing to relinquish some of their control in the classroom. No

matter what we may *say* about wanting students to be more responsible for their learning, we have to back it up with more than rhet-
oric. As Jane Tompkins (1990, p. 656) eloquently reminds us, "The
classroom is a microcosm of the world; it is the chance we have to
practice whatever ideals we may cherish. The kind of classroom
situation one creates is the acid test of what one really stands for."

Yet even for those of us who stand for an approach to teaching in which students take more responsibility for their learning,
a problem remains. The simple fact is that changing one's style of
teaching and modifying settled methods is at best a difficult task.
For changing the ways we teach reaches deeper than merely adopting new teaching strategies. It touches our very identity as teachers.
But if we are willing to work at it, the rewards are forthcoming.
With that in mind, we want to close our book with some practical
suggestions for ways to begin a process of change.

Start Small

Teachers new to active learning should think of small ways to enliven their classrooms by actively involving students. As a simple
beginning, have students write for five minutes on the main points
involved in a reading assignment due for the class period. Then
form small groups of three and ask for a consensus from each group.
Have the groups report back to the class on their findings, listing
points on the blackboard. This bare-bones exercise will take only
fifteen minutes, and it is useful for clarifying confusion and highlighting what students have missed in their reading. It is also an
involving prelude to the day's lecture. Using uncomplicated, low-
risk exercises makes sense before going on to more sophisticated
strategies, such as simulations or cooperative projects.

Know Your Teaching Strengths

This book and the resources we have cited in the Selected Resources
for Additional Reading contain a wide variety of exercises, adaptable to most disciplines. Before experimenting with an exercise in
class, consider how comfortable you will feel guiding your students
through it. Some teachers have a flair for the dramatic and will have

little difficulty using role plays with students. Others may have solid skills for leading classroom discussions. One way to start is by reviewing some of the active-learning strategies outlined in this book to see which ones sound exciting and comfortable or perhaps fit best with the subject you are teaching.

Ask for Help

Before trying a new teaching strategy, find a colleague skilled in that approach and ask about visiting a class to see things firsthand. Most of us are flattered when colleagues want to visit our classes. A colleague might be willing to share teaching materials and help design a small-group exercise or a case study. Some might even come to observe our classes and assess our teaching techniques. This kind of teaching support, or mentoring, has proved quite successful. At our university, we have formalized this visiting and mentoring process in our faculty development program. We know that other institutions have also done this; still others encourage faculty through formalized teaching center activities and workshops.

Expect Some Failures

Teaching is an imprecise venture at best and at times gets messy. Trying out an active-learning strategy for the first time will yield varying degrees of success and failure. Students usually are not nearly as hard on teachers as we are on ourselves, and we should permit ourselves to do a less-than-perfect job the first time around. But after the fact, we need to build on experience—both good and bad—so that next time things will go better. Often the cause of first-time blunders is our lack of clarity in giving instructions. Students need to know exactly what they will be asked to do and why; therefore, we need to figure out those "whats and whys" and translate them for our students as explicitly as possible. Some of the models and instructions we have included throughout this book should help.

Those who think of active learning as a magic cure-all for all our teaching ills are optimists indeed. It is quite likely, in a specific class, that students may not be ready for or amenable to a particular type of active-learning strategy. To be realistic, at times we all end up with that certain classroom of students who just do not respond well to our best efforts. We can try to light the fire of participation under a group of recalcitrant students, but grudging, minimal responses may be our only reward. Our advice is to fight the good fight and look forward to the next opportunity, knowing that a few students will always catch on and appreciate our efforts.

How Will We Know It Works?

How do we know our best-laid plans and teaching efforts are having the intended effect on students? Some assurance in regard to this question certainly would add zest to changing our teaching styles. While we can offer no ironclad guarantees, a few significant indicators are available. First, and most obviously, our students will demonstrate improved mastery over the subject matter. The gap between theory and practice will lessen as they learn to apply that subject matter. And in discussions, exercises, and examinations, we will see how much more they have learned. Next, our classrooms will be livelier places for our students and us as well. Giving students the opportunity to air their concerns and practice using information often results in more and better attention paid to us when the class shifts back to a traditional mode. Increased attendance, more animated discussions, and students' asking questions and hanging around after class are all indicators that active learning is working as a classroom strategy. Though some students may not trust our efforts, if we persist, the end results are generally positive in the majority of attempts.

We will sense our success not only through a more animated classroom, but on a personal level. When we strike off in new directions, teaching often becomes a more invigorating endeavor, for teachers as well as students. Most of us can tell when things are working well and when they are not.

Finally, we can ask students directly how things are going. The work K. Patricia Cross and Thomas A. Angelo have done on classroom research is a profitable starting point. The idea underlying classroom research is "to provide faculty with information and insights into what, how, and how well their particular students are learning in their specific courses" (Angelo, 1991b, p. 8). The point of active learning is not merely to increase motivation and to make learning more plausible, but also to increase the quality of learning. To get at this question of quality, Angelo and Cross propose the use of short, anonymous written exercises called Classroom Assessment Techniques (CATs). CATs can be both a form of active learning and an appraisal of its success. Here's an example.

A technique called Process Self-Analysis offers teachers feedback on what students actually are doing as they work on a particular assignment, but it also could be used to assess how well a new learning strategy is working. For example, three weeks before a final research paper based on cooperative work is due, we can ask our students to spend a couple of minutes writing down on $3'' \times 5''$ cards how well things are going—perhaps in relation to sharing research or outlining the work group's oral presentation. Just asking how things are generally progressing, however, will not yield answers of much value. We need to key our request for written comments to specific aspects of an active-learning activity. The class period after we review the students' written responses is a good time to address issues and concerns.

In *Classroom Assessment Techniques: A Handbook for College Teachers* (1993), Angelo and Cross list fifty different assessment techniques, many of which we can adapt to our concerns about active learning. The key to any assessments we might borrow or create is the immediate information they provide about how things are going. Of course, in using assessments, teachers should consult students on the whats and whys, as well as sharing results with them. Our own observations and intuitions about our teaching are often true, but classroom research adds some "hard data" for us. We should take every opportunity to do this kind of research, because in the process of doing active learning, students and teachers are on constantly shifting sands. Teachers can never assume they know what is going on in their students' minds unless they ask them.

Final Thoughts

Writers inevitably err on the sunny side as they advocate new approaches to teaching and learning. Otherwise, few of us would write. However, it is foolish to imagine that active-learning strategies will immediately change our teaching into the pleasurable activity we all desire. There are always costs as well as benefits to changing a teaching style. For one thing, teachers lose being the center of attention—something most normal people delight in. In departing from the traditional, we hazard frustration and losses, if not outright failures. Still, we have found students to be most forgiving. As we stumble toward a different teaching style, students may see us as human beings after all, and we will lose that cloak of infallibility that teachers wear all too willingly.

Students also lose. They lose the comfort of their well-guarded and long-accepted passivity. Active learning means that they can no longer look on with glazed eyes while their minds wander to other thoughts. And those seasoned professional students can no longer daydream while feigning rapt attention. Students accustomed to the "passive receptacle" approach to learning may not initially welcome active involvement in their education. They remain more or less happy to let someone do it for them.

With all this in mind, we still think the advantages of using active-learning strategies far outweigh the risk of doing nothing at all, especially when we know that learning is more exciting for our students and ourselves. As we admitted at the outset of this book, we are not experts at all these active-learning strategies. In the two years it took to write our book, we have experimented with what are to us very new approaches. We experienced the pain, but also the joy that comes with changing our own teaching. In most cases, our students gave aid and comfort as we tried to change. Part of what they told us, through student evaluations, confirms that they are well on the road to self-directed learning. Many had the opportunity, for the first time, to work with other students in small groups and on cooperative projects. They learned how to appreciate the perspectives and talents of other students. They found that competition for grades is not necessarily what education is all about, nor is it the route toward the best kind of learning. And they found out, as a result of daily practice, more about what a professor of history and philosophy does. What our students have told us, through written evaluations and in-class discussions, is that the classroom is a more hospitable place for them, a place where they can develop their own voice and come to trust their developing academic capabilities.

Most writers like to end their treatises with a few especially well chosen words of wisdom. In the spirit of this book, which drew so heavily on the work of others, we will give the last words to someone else. In his book, *Reaching Out*, Jesuit educator Henri Nouwen (1966, p. 61) says:

> The hospitable teacher has to reveal to the students that they have something to offer. Many students have been for so many years on the receiving side, and have become so deeply impregnated with the idea that there is still a lot more to learn, that they have lost confidence in themselves and can hardly imagine themselves to have something to give. . . . Therefore, the teacher has first of all to reveal, to take away the veil covering many students' intellectual life, and help them see that their own experiences, their own insights and convictions, their own intuitions and formulations are worth serious attention. It is so easy to impress students with books they have not read, with terms that they have not heard, with situations with which they are unfamiliar. It is much more difficult to be a receiver who can help the students distinguish carefully between the wheat and weeds in their own lives and to show the beauty of the gifts they are carrying with them.

Although these are the words of a Jesuit, we will resist saying "Amen." Rather, we will say, "Let us begin."

Selected Resources
For Additional
Reading

For those interested in reading further about the subject of active learning, the literature is abundant and growing. The list of books, articles, and other printed resources contained in this brief section will give readers what we consider important starting points for each of the topics covered in this book. The References in the back of the book offer readers an even wider range of choices for further reading and research.

The Case for Active Learning

As overall surveys of active learning as a field, the various teaching strategies attached to it, and the reasons why this approach makes such good pedagogical sense, we recommend starting with some of the following: Charles C. Bonwell and James A. Eison, *Active Learning: Creating Excitement in the College Classroom*, ASHE-ERIC Higher Education Report no. 1 (Washington, D.C.: The George Washington School of Education and Human Development, 1991); Stephen F. Schomberg (ed.), *Strategies for Active Teaching and Learning in University Classrooms* (Minneapolis: University of Minnesota Press, 1986); Barbara Leigh Smith and Jean T. MacGregor, "What Is Collaborative Learning?" in A. Goodsell, M. Maher, and V. Tinto, with B. L. Smith and J. T. MacGregor, *Collaborative Learning: A Sourcebook for Higher Education* (University Park, Pa.: National Center on Postsecondary

Education, Learning and Assessment, 1992), pp. 9–22; Ohmer Milton and Associates, *On College Teaching: A Guide to Contemporary Practices* (San Francisco: Jossey-Bass, 1978); and Maryellen Weimer, *Improving College Teaching: Strategies for Developing Instructional Effectiveness* (San Francisco: Jossey-Bass, 1990). Wilbert J. McKeachie's *Teaching Tips: A Guidebook for the Beginning College Teacher,* 8th ed. (Lexington, Mass.: Heath, 1986), helps introduce a number of strategies and teaching approaches. Bette LaSere Erickson and Diane Weltner Strommer, *Teaching College Freshmen* (San Francisco: Jossey-Bass, 1991) covers a wide range of issues and subjects with verve and authority.

We also recommend some venerable works that helped frame our ideas about a case for active learning, such as John Dewey, *How We Think* (Heath, [1910] 1982); and Alfred North Whitehead, *The Aims of Education* (New York, Free Press, [1929], 1967). More recent, but ranking as classics, are the books and articles of K. Patricia Cross, Malcolm Knowles, Kenneth Eble, and Parker Palmer listed in the References. James A. Banks, "Ethnicity, Class, Cognitive, and Motivational Styles: Research and Teaching Implications," *Journal of Negro Education,* 1988, *57*(4), 452–466, and Mary B. Belenky, B. M. Clinchy, N. R. Goldberger, and J. M. Tarule, *Women's Ways of Knowing* (New York: Basic Books, 1986) are important for thinking about active learning in terms of diverse student populations and gender issues.

What Active Learning Is and How It Works

The elements we have identified as central to active learning are talking and listening, writing, reading, and reflecting. Here are some resources directly related to those key elements of active learning: Toby Fulwiler, *Teaching with Writing* (Portsmouth, N.H.: Boynton/Cook Publishers, 1987); Jack Mezirow and Associates, *Fostering Critical Reflection in Adulthood: A Guide to Transformative and Emancipatory Learning* (San Francisco: Jossey-Bass, 1990); Stephen D. Brookfield, *The Skillful Teacher: On Technique, Trust, and Responsiveness in the Classroom* (San Francisco: Jossey-Bass, 1990); Walter L. Bateman, *Open to Question: The Art of Teaching and Learning by Inquiry* (San Francisco: Jossey-Bass,

1990); and Richard C. Anderson and P. David Pearson, "A Schematic-Theoretic View of Basic Processes in Reading Comprehension," in P. David Pearson (ed.), *Handbook of Reading Research* (White Plains, N.Y.: Longman, 1984).

Creating an Active-Learning Environment

Preparing to teach in an active-learning environment requires thinking about a range of elements, as diverse as clarifying course objectives and arranging the chairs and desks in a teaching space. William Welty's "Discussion Method Teaching," *Change*, Jul.–Aug. 1989, pp. 41–49, is a very compact, readable overview that covers many of the topics we thought important for Chapter Three. Chet Meyers, *Teaching Students to Think Critically: A Guide for Faculty in All Disciplines* (San Francisco: Jossey-Bass, 1986), especially Chapter Five; Kenneth E. Eble, *The Craft of Teaching: A Guide to Mastering the Professor's Art*, 2nd ed. (San Francisco: Jossey-Bass, 1988); Stephen Scholl-Buckwald, "The First Class Meeting," in Joseph Katz (ed.), *Teaching as Though Students Mattered*, New Directions for Teaching and Learning, no. 21 (San Francisco: Jossey-Bass, 1985); and Arthur W. Chickering and Zelda F. Gamson, "Seven Principles for Good Practice," *AAHE Bulletin*, 1987, *39*, 3–7, offer important suggestions and insights. Bob Magnan (ed.), *147 Practical Tips for Teaching Professors* (Madison, Wis.: Magna Publications, 1989) has conveniently assembled worthwhile tips about a range of classroom situations from the issues of *The Teaching Professor*.

Informal Small Groups

It is difficult to put together just a brief list of resources on informal small groups because so much material is available in books, disciplinary and teaching journals, and newsletters. Here are our choices for those embarking on an introduction to this fundamental strategy for active learning. David Johnson, Roger Johnson, and Karl A. Smith, *Active Learning: Cooperation in the College Classroom* (Edina, Minn.: Interaction Book Company, 1991), Chapter Five, should be a first stop on anyone's reading list. Stephen D. Brookfield's *The Skillful Teacher: On Technique, Trust, and Re-*

sponsiveness in the Classroom (San Francisco: Jossey-Bass, 1990) contains some practical and sensible advice on small groups. Peter J. Frederick's "Student Involvement: Active Learning in Large Classes," in Maryellen Gleason Weimer (ed.). *Teaching Large Classes Well*, New Directions for Teaching and Learning, no. 32 (San Francisco: Jossey-Bass, 1987), explains how to incorporate small-group discussions into large classes. Richard G. Tiberius, *Small Group Teaching: A Trouble Shooting Guide* (Toronto: Ontario Institute for Studies in Education, 1990), is valuable for exactly what the title implies.

Cooperative Student Projects

David Johnson, Roger Johnson, and Karl A. Smith, *Active Learning: Cooperation in the College Classroom* (Edina, Minn.: Interaction Book Company, 1991), proved invaluable for understanding the nature and workings of cooperative student projects. We also recommend two articles by Robert E. Slavin, "Cooperative Learning," *Review of Educational Research*, 1980, *5*(2), 315–342, and "When Does Cooperative Learning Increase Student Achievement?" *Psychological Bulletin*, 1983, *94*(3), 429–445. The relationship between cooperative projects and the learning styles of diverse cultural groups is revealed in James A. Vasquez, "Teaching to Distinctive Traits of Minority Students," *The Clearing House*, 1990, *63* (special edition), 299–304; Lee Little Soldier, "Language Learning of Native American Students," *Educational Leadership*, 1989, *46*(5), 74–75; and C. Skully Stikes, *Black Students in Higher Education* (Carbondale and Edwardsville: Southern Illinois University Press, 1984). For information on cooperative learning and multicultural education, see Nancy Schniedewind and Mara Sapon-Shevin, "Cooperative Learning as Empowering Pedagogy," in Christine Sleeter (ed.), *Empowerment Through Multicultural Education* (Albany: State University of New York Press, 1991), Chapter Seven.

Simulations

Simulations have attracted some especially good research and writing. As a general overview, Terrie M. Shannon, "Introducing Simulation and Role Play," in Stephen F. Schomberg (ed.), *Strategies for Active Learning in University Classrooms* (Minneapolis: University of Minnesota Press, 1986); Dean S. Dorn, "Simulation Games: One More Tool on the Pedagogical Shelf," *Teaching Sociology*, 1989, *17*, 1–18; and Michael J. Rockler, "Applying Simulation/Gaming," in Ohmer Milton and Associates, *On College Teaching: A Guide to Contemporary Practices* (San Francisco: Jossey-Bass, 1978), are excellent. Ronald T. Hyman, *Using Simulation Games in the College Classroom*, Idea Paper no. 5 (Manhattan: Center for Faculty Evaluation and Development, Kansas State University, Apr. 1981), surveys the use of simulation games in the classroom.

Case Studies

John Boehrer and Marty Linsky's article "Teaching with Cases: Learning to Question," in Marilla D. Svinicki (ed.), *The Changing Face of College Teaching*, New Directions for Teaching and Learning, no. 42 (San Francisco: Jossey-Bass, 1990), and Charles F. Fisher, "Being There Vicariously by Case Studies," in Ohmer Milton and Associates, *On College Teaching: A Guide to Contemporary Practices* (San Francisco: Jossey-Bass, 1978), clearly translate a broad and complex subject. These articles are a good introduction for reading the Harvard Business School publications, such as the engaging and informative book by C. Roland Christensen, David A. Garvin, and Ann Sweet (eds.), *Education for Judgment: The Artistry of Discussion Leadership* (Boston: Harvard Business School Press, 1991), and C. Roland Christensen and Abby J. Hansen, *Teaching and the Case Method* (Boston: Harvard Business School Press, 1987).

Integrating Reading Materials and Guest Speakers

Practical discussions of reading assignments and outside resource persons for the active-learning classroom are hard to find. Many ideas must come in bits and pieces from books and articles on teaching, discussion techniques, and study skills. Readers should refer to Wilbert McKeachie, *Teaching Tips: A Guidebook for the Beginning College Teacher*, 8th ed. (Lexington, Mass.: Heath, 1986); Peter J. Frederick, "The Dreaded Discussion: Ten Ways to Start," in Maryellen Gleason Weimer and Rose Ann Neff (eds.), *Classroom Communication: Collected Readings for Effective Discussion and Questioning* (Madison, Wis.: Magna Publications, 1989); Peter J. Frederick, "The Lively Lecture—Eight Variations," *College Teaching*, 1987, *34*, 43–50; and Thomas G. Devine, *Teaching Study Skills: A Guide for Teachers* (Needham Heights, Mass.: Allyn & Bacon, 1981). Joseph D. Novak and D. Bob Gowan, *Learning How to Learn* (New York: Cambridge University Press, 1984), is a useful introduction to concept mapping, as is Debbie Guice Longman and Rhonda Holt Atkinson, *College Learning and Study Skills* (Saint Paul, Minn.: West Publishing, 1991), Chapter Four.

Using Technology Effectively

In considering the use of teaching technologies in the active-learning classroom, these general surveys are most useful: Barbara Schneider Fuhrman and Anthony Grasha, *A Practical Handbook for College Teachers* (Boston: Little, Brown, 1983), Chapter Nine; Jerome Johnston, *Electronic Learning: From Audiotape to Videodisc* (Hillsdale, N.J.: Erlbaum, 1987); and Ann Kaplan-Neher, *Teaching with Computers* (Sunnyvale, Calif.: PUBLIX Communications, 1991). Critical viewing of television and films is an important topic that readers will want to consider. As introductions, we recommend Stephen D. Brookfield, "Media Power and the Development of Media Literacy: An Adult Educational Interpretation," *Harvard Educational Review*, 1986, *56*(2), 151–170; I. M. Hefzallah, *Critical Viewing of Television* (Lanham, Md.: University Press of America, 1987); Gavriel Salomon, *Interaction of Media, Cognition, and Learning: An Exploration of How Symbolic Forms Cultivate Mental Skills and Affect Knowledge Acquisition* (San Francisco: Jossey-Bass, 1979); and John E. O'Connor, *Teaching History with Film and Television*, Discussions on Teaching (Washington, D.C.: American Historical Association, 1987). For readers starting to investigate the use of microcomputers and other closely linked technology in teaching, we recommend articles carried in journals, magazines, and newsletters such as the *Chronicle of Education*, *Higher Education Product Companion* (**PUBLIX** Information

Products), *T.H.E. Journal: Technological Horizons in Education, EDUCOM Review,* and *Syllabus.* James B. M. Schick's *Teaching History with a Computer: A Complete Guide* (Chicago: Lyceum, 1990) proved a very sensible introduction for more than just historians.

Developing and Assessing Instructional Expertise

Charles C. Bonwell and James A. Eison, *Active Learning: Creating Excitement in the College Classroom,* ASHE-ERIC Higher Education Report no. 1 (Washington, D.C.: The George Washington School of Education and Human Development, 1991), have a very useful concluding section in their book, "Barriers to Change in the Classroom." Thomas A. Angelo and K. Patricia Cross, *Classroom Assessment Techniques: A Handbook for College Teachers,* 2nd ed. (San Francisco: Jossey-Bass, 1993), and Thomas A. Angelo, *Classroom Research: Early Lessons from Success,* New Directions for Teaching and Learning, no. 46 (San Francisco: Jossey-Bass, 1991), deal with ways in which teachers can take steps to know if classroom strategies for active learning are working. Along those lines, we also suggest Maryellen Weimer, Joan L. Parrett, and Mary-Margaret Kerns, *How Am I Teaching? Forms and Activities for Acquiring Instructional Input* (Madison, Wis.: Magna Publications, 1988).

We also gained a great deal from reading issues of journals such as *College Teaching, The Teaching Professor,* and *Change* for an overview of what is taking place in the field of active learning and for specific, practical information on teaching strategies.

References

Adler, M. "How to Mark a Book." *Saturday Review*, July 6, 1940, pp. 11–12.

Anderson, C. J. "Enrollment by Age: Distinguishing the Numbers from the Rates." *Research Briefs*, 1990, *1*(7), 1–8.

Anderson, R. C., and Pearson, P. D. "A Schematic-Theoretic View of Basic Processes in Reading Comprehension." In P. D. Pearson (ed.), *Handbook of Reading Research*. White Plains, N.Y.: Longman, 1984.

Angelo, T. A. "Bridging the Gap Between Education Research and College Teaching." *Faculty Development*, 1991a, *4*(2), 1–3.

Angelo, T. A. *Classroom Research: Early Lessons from Success.* New Directions for Teaching and Learning, no. 46. San Francisco: Jossey-Bass, 1991b.

Angelo, T. A., and Cross, K. P. *Classroom Assessment Techniques: A Handbook for College Teachers.* (2nd ed.) San Francisco: Jossey-Bass, 1993.

Banks, J. A. "Ethnicity, Class, Cognitive, and Motivational Styles; Research and Teaching Implications." *Journal of Negro Education*, 1988, *57*(4), 452–466.

Belenky, M. B., Clinchy, B. M., Goldberger, N. R., and Tarule, J. M. *Women's Ways of Knowing*. New York: Basic Books, 1986.

Bligh, D. A. *What's the Use of Lectures?* Hammondworth, England: Penguin Book, 1972.

Boehrer, J., and Linsky, M. "Teaching with Cases: Learning to Question." In M. D. Svinicki (ed.), *The Changing Face of College Teaching*. New Directions for Teaching and Learning, no. 42. San Francisco: Jossey-Bass, 1990.

Bok, D. "Looking into Education's High-Tech Future." *Harvard Magazine,* 1985, *87,* 2-17.

Borreson, C. R. "Success in Introductory Statistics with Small Groups." *College Teaching,* 1990, *38*(1), 26-28.

Boseker, B. J., and Gordon, S. L. "What Native Americans Have Taught Us as Teacher Educators." *Journal of American Indian Education,* May 1983, pp. 20-24.

Bouton, C., and Garth, R. Y. "Students in Learning Groups: Active Learning Through Conversation." In C. Bouton and R. Y. Garth (eds.), *Learning in Groups.* New Directions for Teaching and Learning, no. 14. San Francisco: Jossey-Bass, 1983.

Bowen, D. D. "Developing a Personal Theory of Experiential Learning: A Dispatch from the Trenches." *Simulation and Games,* 1987, *18*(2), 192-206.

Bransford, J. D. *Human Cognition: Learning, Understanding, and Remembering.* Belmont, Calif.: Wadsworth, 1979.

Briggs-Myers, I. *Gifts Differing.* Palo Alto, Calif.: Consulting Psychologists Press, 1980.

Brookfield, S. D. "Media Power and the Development of Media Literacy: An Adult Educational Interpretation." *Harvard Educational Review,* 1986, *56*(2), 151-170.

Brookfield, S. D. *Developing Critical Thinkers: Challenging Adults to Explore Alternative Ways of Thinking and Acting.* San Francisco: Jossey-Bass, 1987.

Brookfield, S. D. *The Skillful Teacher: On Technique, Trust, and Responsiveness in the Classroom.* San Francisco: Jossey-Bass, 1990.

Browne, D. B., and Bordeau, L. "How South Dakota Teachers See Learning Style Differences." *Tribal College,* 1991, *2*(4), 24-26.

Bruffee, K. "Collaborative Learning and the Conversation of Mankind." *College English,* 1984, *46*(7), 635-652.

Bruffee, K. "The Art of Collaborative Learning." *Change,* Mar.-Apr. 1987, pp. 42-47.

The Case Method. Prepared by the Philippine Case Clearing House and distributed by the Intercollegiate Case Clearing House, Soldiers Field, Boston, 1969.

Cashin, W. E. *Improving Lectures.* Idea Paper no. 14. Manhattan:

Center for Faculty Evaluation and Development, Kansas State University, Sept. 1985.

Charlesworth, W. R. "Introducing Active Learning: Conceptual and Practical Problems." In S. F. Schomberg (ed.), *Strategies for Active Teaching and Learning in University Classrooms.* Minneapolis: University of Minnesota Press, 1986, p. 11–17.

Chickering, A. W., and Gamson, Z. F. "Seven Principles for Good Practice." *AAHE Bulletin,* 1987, *39,* 3–7.

Christensen, C. R., Garvin, D. A., and Sweet, A. (eds.). *Education for Judgment: The Artistry of Discussion Leadership.* Boston: Harvard Business School Press, 1991.

Christensen, C. R., and Hansen, A. J. *Teaching and the Case Method.* Boston: Harvard Business School Press, 1987.

Christensen, C. R., Hansen, A. J., and Moore, J. F. *Teaching and the Case Method: Instructor's Guide.* Boston: Harvard Business School Press, 1987.

Cloud, B., and Sweeny, J. "Effective Guest Speakers Require Care and Thought." *Journalism Educator,* 1988, *42,* 30–31.

Corder, J. "Traditional Lectures Still Have a Place in the Classroom." *The Chronicle of Higher Education,* June 12, 1991, p. B2.

Cross, K. P. "Every Teacher a Researcher, Every Classroom a Laboratory." In *Tribal College: A Journal of American Indian Higher Education,* Spring 1991, *2*(4), 7–12.

Devine, T. G. *Teaching Study Skills: A Guide for Teachers.* Needham Heights, Mass.: Allyn & Bacon, 1981.

Dewey, J. *How We Think.* Lexington, Mass.: Heath, 1982. (Originally published 1910.)

Dorn, D. S. "Simulation Games: One More Tool on the Pedagogical Shelf." *Teaching Sociology,* 1989, *17,* 1–18.

Duckworth, E. "The Having of Wonderful Ideas." *Harvard Educational Review,* 1972, *42*(2), 217–231.

Eble, K. E. *The Aims of College Teaching.* San Francisco: Jossey-Bass, 1983.

Eble, K. E. *The Craft of Teaching: A Guide to Mastering the Professor's Art.* (2nd ed.) San Francisco: Jossey-Bass, 1988.

Eison, J., and Bonwell, C. "Making Real the Promise of Active Learning." Paper presented at the 1988 National Conference of the American Association of Higher Education, Washington,

D.C., Mar. 9-12, 1988. Available through the Center for Teaching and Learning, Southeast Missouri State University, Cape Girardeau, Mo. 63701.

Elmore, R. F. "Foreword." In C. R. Christensen, D. A. Garvin, and A. Sweet (eds.), *Education for Judgment: The Artistry of Discussion Leadership.* Boston: Harvard Business School Press, 1991.

Emig, J. "Writing as a Mode of Learning." *College Composition and Communication,* 1977, *28,* 122-128.

Erickson, B. L., and Strommer, D. W. *Teaching College Freshmen.* San Francisco: Jossey-Bass, 1991.

Erickson, S. C. *The Essence of Good Teaching: Helping Students Learn and Remember What They Learn.* San Francisco: Jossey-Bass, 1984.

Fisher, C. F. "Being There Vicariously by Case Studies." In O. Milton and Associates, *On College Teaching: A Guide to Contemporary Practices.* San Francisco: Jossey-Bass, 1978.

Frederick, P. J. "The Lively Lecture—Eight Variations." *College Teaching,* 1987a, *34,* 43-50.

Frederick, P. J. "Student Involvement: Active Learning in Large Classes." In M. G. Weimer (ed.), *Teaching Large Classes Well.* New Directions for Teaching and Learning. no. 32. San Francisco: Jossey-Bass, 1987b, pp. 45-56.

Frederick, P. J. "The Dreaded Discussion: Ten Ways to Start." In M. G.. Weimer and R. A. Neff (eds.), *Classroom Communication: Collected Readings for Effective Discussion and Questioning.* Madison, Wis.: Magna Publications, 1989.

Fulwiler, T. *Teaching with Writing.* Portsmouth, N.H.: Boynton/Cook Publishers, 1987.

Gaede, H. L. "When They Don't Do the Reading." *Teaching Professor,* 1989, *3,* 4.

Gilligan, C. *In a Different Voice.* Cambridge, Mass: Harvard University Press, 1982.

Ginsberg, H., and Oper, S. *Piaget's Theory of Intellectual Development: An Introduction.* Englewood Cliffs, N.J.: Prentice-Hall, 1969.

Greenblatt, C. S. *Designing Games and Simulations.* Newbury Park, Calif.: Sage, 1987.

Greenwald, B. "Teaching Technical Material." In C. R. Christensen, D. A. Garvin, and A. Sweet (eds.), *Education for Judgment: The Artistry of Discussion Leadership.* Boston: Harvard Business School Press, 1991, pp. 193-214.

Guild, P. B., and Garger, S. *Marching to Different Drummers.* Alexandria, Va.: Association for Supervision and Curriculum Development, 1985.

Hansen, A. J. "Reflections of a Case Writer: Writing Teaching Cases." In C. R. Christensen, *Teaching and the Case Method.* Boston: Harvard Business School Press, 1987, pp. 264-270.

Hefzallah, I. M. *Critical Viewing of Television.* Lanham, Md.: University Press of America, 1987.

How to Run Better Business Meetings: A Reference Guide for Managers. New York: McGraw-Hill, 1987.

Hunt, M. *The Universe Within: A New Science Explores the Human Mind.* New York: Simon & Schuster, 1982.

Hutchings, P. "Assessment and the Way It Works." Closing plenary address, Fifth American Association of Higher Education Conference on Assessment, Washington, D.C., June 30, 1990.

Hyman, R. T. *Using Simulation Games in the College Classroom.* Idea Paper no. 5. Manhattan: Center for Faculty Evaluation and Development, Kansas State University, Apr. 1981.

"Interactive Videodisks of Film Help Students Learn Foreign Languages." *The Chronicle of Higher Education,* Oct. 23, 1991, pp. A18-A20.

Jacobson, R. L. "Asking Questions Is the Key Skill Needed for 'Discussion Teaching.'" *The Chronicle of Higher Education,* July 25, 1984, pp. 17, 20.

Johnson, D., Johnson, R., and Johnson Holubec, E. *Circles of Learning.* (3rd ed.) Edina, Minn.: Interaction Book Company, 1990.

Johnson, D., Johnson, R., and Smith, K. A. "Cooperative Learning: An Active Learning Strategy." *FOCUS on Teaching and Learning,* 1990, 5(2), 1, 7-8.

Johnson, D., Johnson, R., and Smith, K. A. *Active Learning: Cooperation in the College Classroom.* Edina, Minn.: Interaction Book Company, 1991.

Johnson, D., and others. "Effects of Cooperative and Individualistic

Goal Structures on Achievement: A Meta-Analysis." *Psychological Bulletin*, 1981, *89*(1), 47–62.

Jones, K. *Designing Your Own Simulations.* London: Methuen, 1985.

Jones, K. *Interactive Learning Events: A Guide for Facilitators.* London: Kogan Page, 1988.

Jones, L. L., and Smith, S. G. "Can Multimedia Instruction Meet Our Expectations?" *EDUCOM Review*, 1992, *27*(1), 39–43.

Kagan, N. "Influencing Human Interaction: Interpersonal Process Recall (IPR) Stimulated by Videotape." In O. Zubar-Skerritt (ed.), *Video in Higher Education*. London: Kogan Page, 1984, pp. 93–113.

Kleinfeld, J. S. *Instructional Style and the Intellectual Development of Village Indian and Eskimo Students*. Washington, D.C.: U.S. Office of Education, 1972.

Klemer, R., and Smith, R. *Teaching About Family Relationships*. Minneapolis, Minn.: Burgess, 1975.

Knowles, M. *The Modern Practice of Adult Education*. (Rev. ed.) Chicago: Follett, 1980.

Kohlberg, L. "Stage and Sequence: The Cognitive-Developmental Approach to Socialization." In D. A. Goslin (ed.), *Handbook of Socialization Theory and Research*. Skokie, Ill.: Rand McNally, 1969.

Kolb, D. A. *Experiential Learning: Experience as a Source of Learning and Development*. Englewood Cliffs, N.J.: Prentice-Hall, 1984.

Kozma, R. B., and Johnston, J. "The Technological Revolution Comes to the Classroom." *Change*, Jan.–Feb. 1991, pp. 10–23.

Kraft, R. G. "Group Inquiry Turns Passive Students Active." *College Teaching*, 1985, *33*, 149–154.

Lane, K. "Using Actors as 'Clients' for an Interviewing Simulation in an Undergraduate Psychology Course." *Teaching of Psychology*, 1988, *15*, 162–164.

Larkin, J., and Simon, H. "Why a Diagram is (Sometimes) Worth Ten Thousand Words." *Cognitive Science*, 1987, *11*, 65–99.

Lawson, A., and Renner, J. "Piagetian Theory and Biology Teaching." *The American Biology Teacher*, 1975, *37*(6), 336–343.

Little Soldier, L. "Language Learning of Native American Students." *Educational Leadership,* 1989, *46*(5), 74–75.

Lochhead, J., and Whimbey, A. "Teaching Analytical Reasoning Through Thinking Aloud Pair Problem Solving." In J. E. Stice (ed.), *Developing Critical Thinking and Problem-Solving Abilities.* New Directions for Teaching and Learning, no. 30. San Francisco: Jossey-Bass, 1987.

Longman, D. G., and Atkinson, R. H. *College Learning and Study Skills.* Saint Paul, Minn.: West Publishing, 1991.

Lukinsky, J. "Reflective Withdrawal Through Journal Writing." In J. Mezirow and Associates, *Fostering Critical Reflection in Adulthood: A Guide to Transformative and Anticipatory Learning.* San Francisco: Jossey-Bass, 1990.

Lynch, P. "Multimedia in Higher Education." *Higher Education Product Companion,* 1992, *1*(2), 20–26.

Maas, J. "Reflections on Discussion Teaching: An Interview with C. Roland Christensen." *Harvard Business Publications Newsletter.* Fall 1991, pp. 1–6.

McKeachie, W. J. *Teaching Tips: A Guidebook for the Beginning College Teacher.* (8th ed.) Lexington, Mass.: Heath, 1986.

McNeil, L. D. "Logging the Interpretive Act: Dialogue in the Literature Classroom." *College Teaching,* 1988, *37*(3), 86–90.

Meyers, C. *Teaching Students to Think Critically: A Guide for Faculty in All Disciplines.* San Francisco: Jossey-Bass, 1986.

Mezirow, J., and Associates. *Fostering Critical Reflection in Adulthood: A Guide to Transformative and Emancipatory Learning.* San Francisco: Jossey-Bass, 1990.

Myers, A. D., and Weeks, L. "Writing and Teaching Cases." In H. R. Bridston, F. Foulkes, A. D. Myers, and L. Weeks (eds.), *Casebook on Church and Society.* Nashville, Tenn. Abington Press, 1974.

National Center for Education Statistics. "Trends in Racial/Ethnic Enrollment in Higher Education: Fall 1980 Through Fall 1990." Tabulated by N. B. Schantz. Washington, D.C.: U.S. Department of Education, 1992.

National Commission on Education. *A Nation At Risk.* Washington, D.C.: U.S. Department of Education, 1983.

Nouwen, H. *Reaching Out.* New York: Doubleday, 1966.

Novak, J. D., and Gowin, D. B. *Learning How to Learn*. New York: Cambridge University Press, 1984.

Nyquist, J. D., and Wulff, D. H. "Selected Active Learning Strategies." In J. Daly, G. Friedrich, and A. Vangelisti (eds.), *Teaching Communication: Theory, Research, and Methods*. Hillsdale, N.J.: Erlbaum, 1990, pp. 337–362.

O'Connor, J. E. *Teaching History with Film and Television*. Discussions on Teaching. Washington, D.C.: American Historical Association, 1987.

Palmer, J., and Snyder, T.F.F. "Computer Simulations Come of Age." In L. H. Lewis (ed.), *Experiential and Simulation Techniques for Teaching Adults*. New Directions for Adult & Continuing Education, no. 30. San Francisco: Jossey-Bass, 1986.

Palmer, P. J. "Community, Conflict, and Ways of Knowing." *Change*, 1987, *19*(5), 20–25.

Perry, W. *Forms of Intellectual and Ethical Development in the College Years: A Scheme*. Troy, Mo.: Holt, Rinehart & Winston, 1970.

Piaget, J. *The Psychology of Intelligence*. Totowa, N.J.: Littlefield Adams, 1976.

Pintrich, P. "Student Learning and College Teaching." In R. E. Young and K. E. Eble (eds.), *College Teaching and Learning: Preparing for New Commitments*. New Directions for Teaching and Learning, no. 33. San Francisco: Jossey-Bass, 1988.

Pollio, H. R. *What Students Think About and Do in College Lecture Classes*. Teaching-Learning Issues no. 53. Knoxville: Learning Research Center, University of Tennessee, 1984.

Postman, N. "Critical Thinking in the Electronic Era." *National Forum*, 1985, *65*(1), 4–8, 17.

Ramírez, M., and Castañeda, A. *Cultural Democracy, Bicognitive Development in Education*. San Diego, Calif.: Academic Press, 1974.

Rich, S. U. "Business School Objectives and the Case Method of Teaching." Distributed by Intercollegiate Case Clearing House, Soldier's Field, Boston, 1969.

Rickard, H., Rogers, R., Ellis, N., and Beidleman, W. "Some Retention, But Not Enough." *Teaching of Psychology*, 1988, *15*, 151–152.

Rockler, M. J. "Applying Simulation/Gaming." In O. Milton and Associates, *On College Teaching: A Guide to Contemporary Practices*. San Francisco: Jossey-Bass, 1978.

Salomon, G. *Interaction of Media, Cognition, and Learning: An Exploration of How Symbolic Forms Cultivate Mental Skills and Affect Knowledge Acquisition*. San Francisco: Jossey-Bass, 1979.

Schick, J.B.M. *Teaching History with a Computer: A Complete Guide*. Chicago: Lyceum, 1990.

Schniedewind, N., and Sapon-Shevin, M. "Cooperative Learning as Empowering Pedagogy." In Sleeter, C. (ed.), *Empowerment Through Multicultural Education*. Albany: State University of New York Press, 1991, chap. 7.

Scholl-Buckwald, S. "The First Class Meeting." In Joseph Katz (ed.), *Teaching as Though Students Mattered*. New Directions for Teaching and Learning, no. 21. San Francisco: Jossey-Bass, 1985.

Schön, D. A. *Educating the Reflective Practitioner: Toward a New Design for Teaching and Learning in the Professions*. San Francisco: Jossey-Bass, 1987.

Scott, L. U., and Heller, P. "Team Work: Strategies for Integrating Women and Minorities into the Physical Sciences." *The Science Teacher*, 1991, *58*, 24–27.

Sedlack, M. W., Wheeler, C. W., Pallin, D. C., and Gusick, P. A. *Selling Students Short: Classroom Bargains and Academic Reform in the American High School*. New York: Teachers College Press, 1986.

Shannon, T. M. "Introducing Simulation and Role Play." In S. F. Schomberg (ed.), *Strategies for Active Learning in University Classrooms*. Minneapolis: University of Minnesota Press, 1986.

Sharan, S. "Cooperative Learning in Small Groups: Recent Methods and Effects on Achievement, Attitudes, and Ethnic Relations." *Review of Educational Research*, 1980, *50*(2), 241–271.

Sheridan, J., Bryne, A. C., and Quina, K. "Collaborative Learning: Notes from the Field." *College Teaching*, 1989, *37*(2), 49–53.

Slavin, R. E. "Cooperative Learning." *Review of Educational Research*, 1980, *5*(2), 315–342.

Slavin, R. E. "When Does Cooperative Learning Increase Student Achievement?" *Psychological Bulletin*, 1983, *94*(3), 429–445.

"Slow Down, You Move Too Fast." *Phi Delta Kappan,* 1987, *69,* 234.

Smith, B. L., and MacGregor, J. T. "What Is Collaborative Learning?" in A. Goodsell, M. Maher, and V. Tinto, with B. L. Smith and J. T. MacGregor, *Collaborative Learning: A Sourcebook for Higher Education.* University Park, Pa.: National Center on Postsecondary Education, Learning and Assessment, 1992.

Stevenson, L. *Seven Theories of Human Nature.* (Rev. ed.) New York: Oxford University Press, 1987.

Stice, J. E. "Further Reflections: Useful Resources." In J. E. Stice (ed.), *Developing Critical Thinking and Problem-Solving Abilities.* New Directions for Teaching and Learning, no. 30. San Francisco: Jossey-Bass, 1987.

Stikes, C. S. *Black Students in Higher Education.* Carbondale and Edwardsville: Southern Illinois University Press, 1984.

Tiberius, R. G. "Metaphors Underlying the Improvement of Teaching and Learning." *British Journal of Educational Technology,* 1986, *17*(2), 144–156.

Tompkins, J. "Pedagogy of the Distressed." *College English,* 1990, *52*(6), 653–660.

Vasquez, J. A. "Teaching to Distinctive Traits of Minority Students." *The Clearing House,* 1990, *63* (special ed.), 299–304.

Verner, C. and Dickinson, G. "The Lecture: An Analysis and Review of Research." *Adult Education,* 1967, *17*(2), 85–90.

Weimer, M. *Improving College Teaching: Strategies for Developing Instructional Effectiveness.* San Francisco: Jossey-Bass, 1990.

Weimer, M. G. (ed.). *Teaching Large Classes Well.* New Directions for Teaching and Learning, no. 32. San Francisco: Jossey-Bass, 1987.

Weimer, M. G., and Neff, R. A. (eds.). *Classroom Communication: Collected Readings for Effective Discussion and Questioning.* Madison, Wis.: Magna Publications, 1989.

Weiner, H. "Collaborative Learning in the Classroom: A Guide to Evaluation." *College English,* 1986, *48*(1), 52–61.

Weinstein, C. E., Goetz, E. T., and Alexander, P. *Learning and Study Strategies: Issues in Assessment.* San Diego, Calif.: Academic Press, 1988.

Welty, W. M. "Discussion Method Teaching." *Change,* Jul.-Aug. 1989, pp. 41-49.

Whimbey, A., and others. "Teaching Critical Reading and Analytical Reasoning in Project SOAR." *Journal of Reading,* Oct. 1980, *24*(1), pp. 5-10.

Whitehead, A. N. *The Aims of Education.* New York: Free Press, 1967. (Originally published 1929.)

Winograd, P., and Hare, V. C. "Direct Instruction of Reading Comprehension Strategies: The Nature of Teacher Explanation." In C. E. Weinstein, E. T. Goetz, and P. A. Alexander (eds.), *Learning and Study Strategies: Issues in Assessment, Instruction, and Evaluation.* San Diego, Calif.: Academic Press, pp. 121-139.

Wulff, D. H., Nyquist, J. D., and Abbott, R. D. "Students' Perceptions of Large Classes." In M. G. Weimer (ed.), *Teaching Large Classes Well.* New Directions for Teaching and Learning, no. 32. San Francisco: Jossey-Bass, 1987.

Zinsser, W. *Writing to Learn.* New York: HarperCollins, 1988.

Index